NEWLY REVISED AND UPDATED

THE COMPLETE GUIDE TO REAL ESTATE LOANS

NEWLY REVISED AND UPDATED

THE COMPLETE GUIDE TO REAL ESTATE LOANS

ANDREW JAMES McLEAN

Contemporary Books, Inc.
Chicago

For the purposes of simplicity and easier understanding the author has employed the use of the noun "mortgage" to represent both deeds of trust and mortgages throughout this text. Although both instruments are very similar, technically there is a difference. Due to the fact that half the country uses a mortgage for a security instrument while the remainder uses a deed of trust, it makes this text less complicated when only one of these instruments is continually referred to.

Published by Contemporary Books, Inc.
180 North Michigan Avenue, Chicago, Illinois 60601
Manufactured in the United States of America
International Standard Book Number: 0-8092-5471-9

Published simultaneously in Canada by Beaverbooks, Ltd.
195 Allstate Parkway, Valleywood Business Park
Markham, Ontario L3R 4T8 Canada

WHY SHOULD YOU READ THIS BOOK?

During the past two decades tremendous changes have taken place in the real estate marketplace. Prior to this period interest rates were relatively stable while real estate prices escalated only moderately. But during the past twenty years interest rates have soared to record highs and accordingly have affected the value of real property.

It was during this highly volatile period that many homeowners and potential home buyers were either hampered from purchasing a new home because of these excessive interest rates, or, if they were able to buy their new home, they were penalized with a costly high interest rate loan for thirty years. Those who applied for a new loan at the ridiculous rate of 18% and were turned down perhaps were unaware that many other sources of real estate financing were available at half the going rate of 18%. And for those who applied for those expensive loans and got them, now that interest rates have subsided to below 12%, the question remains of how to get out from under the burdensome loans.

For the potential new home buyer who doesn't want to pay an excessive rate of interest and whose credit is less than a perfect "A-One," the best bargain in a home purchase is a VA or FHA loan assumption. This method of financing requires no credit qualifying by the buyer, and he assumes a low interest rate loan which was initiated years earlier by the seller of the property.

The text you are about to read is a comprehensive guide written to assist the consumer in the purchase of a future home or investment property or in the refinancing of an existing property.

With today's sophisticated variable rates and graduated payment mortages, there is a definite need by the consumer to know and understand the lending market that functions to accommodate the home buyer. This is accomplished by being acquainted with the most common methods of financing real property and familiarizing oneself with the terminology used in the world of real estate finance.

Beginning with a description of money and interest rates, the book illustrates a variety of sources for real estate funding including refinancing or taking out a second mortgage to buy additional property. Also, comprehensive guides to various financial instruments, VA and FHA financing, the in's and out's of assumption, taking subject to a mortgage, and the all-inclusive trust deed are thoroughly discussed. The text concludes by covering the topics of financial disclosure, figuring yield, leverage and borrowed money.

The importance of finance should not be underestimated because it is the tool that enables the potential investor to acquire either a home for his family, or an abundance of investment property.

According to statistics, approximately one-third of American families own their home. About 14% of all Americans own more than one home. These figures may not sound that startling for a country referred to as "the land of opportunity," but if compared to home ownership in Europe, one can see that Americans are much better off.

Methods of home finance in European countries require the buyer to furnish a down payment of one-third or more of the purchase price, while interest rates recently have exceeded 18%. It is no wonder that only a mere 10% of European families own their own home.

In the United States, requirements for home financing are far less stringent. Conventional loans offer 80% financing while government loans demand much less of an investment by the potential home buyer.

While today's seemingly high interest rates for home loans appear to have no end, in reality, they are a bargain at today's rate of 12%.

You may wonder how I arrived at such a conclusion. With a 12% mortgage, today's home buyer is actually paying about 1.64%. This is due to the fact that a married couple with a taxable income of $20,000, and an income tax rate of 28%, reduces its effective rate of interest from the prevailing 12% to 8.64% by virtue of the tax deductibility of the interest (12% less 28% of 12 equals 8.64%). Then, this figure can be reduced further to 1.64% by deducting a moderate 7% rate of inflation.

When the rate of inflation is in excess of 7%, the couple may actually be paying zero or a negative rate of interest.

Twenty years ago, a couple buying a home with a 6% mortgage, and in the then lower 14% tax bracket, would have an effective interest rate reduced to about 5.16% (6% less .84% equals 5.16%).Consider then, a 2% rate of inflation, the couple was actually paying 3.16%, or almost 50% more than the comparable 1.64% rate prevailing today.

Obviously, this 12% interest rate appears to be a bargain . . . and it is no wonder as real estate continues to be the best form of investment available.

Real estate has proven itself to be the best hedge against inflation. Since the Great Depression of 1929, real estate values on the average have appreciated one-and-a-half times that of the rate of inflation during the same time period.

This fact is further evidenced by the growing number of home buyers who are willing to burden themselves with historically high interest rates. This new breed of "homebuyer-investors" are thinking like shrewd businessmen. When borrowing to buy more during these times of double-digit inflation, a wise businessman can realistically expect his asset value to increase and that he will be repaying the debt with deflated dollars of the future.

Due to the soaring real estate prices complimented by less land available for housing, developers are shifting their building emphasis from single family homes to high density condominiums. At the same time the trend of the average American family is toward both husband and wife working while maintaining a smaller family. Since this contemporary family requires less livable space, the idea of a more affordable condominium fits right in with their needs.

Aside from the onslaught of condominium construction sprouting up all over the countryside, significant changes in the future of home financing can be expected. To accommodate the potential home-buying public, lenders are beginning to offer more flexible forms of financing including variable rates and graduate payment mortgages. Further changes by lenders may be in the offering in order to allow more families to afford the high cost of home ownership. This is likely to be in the form of extended term financing, perhaps 40 or 50 year mortgages, as opposed to the current 30 year term.

While inflation and rising rates of interest appear to be eroding purchasing power, real estate holdings continue to appreciate at a much faster rate. It is important to remember that real estate values have increased at a rate one-and-a-half times the rate of inflation. Therefore, before putting off a new purchase because of high mortgage rates, consider that delaying the purchase of property will cost appreciably more later.

CONTENTS

WHY SHOULD YOU READ THIS BOOK? *7*
THE MONEY SUPPLY AND INTEREST RATE *15*
The Money Supply *15*
Interest Rates *16*
INTEREST *21*
Simple Interest *21*
360 Days vs. 365 Days *24*
Odd Days Interest *26*
Remaining Balance and Balloon Payment *26*
Add-On Interest *27*
Compound Interest *28*
Comparing Add-On to Simple Interest Loans *28*
SOURCES OF REAL ESTATE FINANCING *31*
Savings and Loan Associations *31*
Mutual Savings Banks *32*
Commercial Banks *33*
Insurance Companies *33*
Credit Unions *34*
Private Mortgage Insurance *34*
Mortgage Bankers *34*
Mortgage Companies *35*
Home Loan Companies *35*
Loan Brokers *35*
Existing Sellers *38*
Functioning of the Money Market *38*
How to Borrow Money *39*
Should You Refinance or Take Out a Second Loan? *41*

FINANCIAL INSTRUMENTS AND LOANS *45*
Financial Instruments *45*
Open-End Mortgages *46*
Construction Mortgages *47*
Mortgages with Release Clauses *47*
Foreclosure *48*
Land Contract *51*
Acceleration Clause *53*
Prepayment *54*
Other Types of Loans *54*
LOAN COMMITMENTS *57*
Future Commitment *57*
Forward Loan Commitment *58*
Take-out Commitments *59*
Permanent Loan Commitment *59*
FEDERAL HOUSING ADMINISTRATION (FHA) FINANCING *61*
FHA Programs Covered *61*
FHA TITLE-II Sec. 203(b)—One to Four Family Dwellings *62*
FHA TITLE II-Sec. 203(b)—Veterans *67*
FHA TITLE II-Sec. 207—Rental Housing & Mobile Home Parks *68*
FHA TITLE II-Sec. 221(d)(4)—Rental Housing *69*
FHA TITLE II-Sec. 221(d)(2)—Rehabilitation of Low Cost Housing *71*
FHA TITLE II-Sec. 222—Loans For In-Service Personnel *72*
FHA TITLE II-Sec. 223(f)—Existing Multi-family Buildings *73*
FHA TITLE II-Sec. 234(c)—Condominiums *74*
FHA TITLE II-Sec. 234(d)—Condominium Projects *74*
FHA TITLE II-Sec. 235—Low Cost Housing Assistance *76*

FHA Sec. 245—Graduated Payment Mortgage (GPM) *78*
FHA TITLE I—Mobile Homes *83*
Purpose *83*
Restrictions *83*
Loans *83*
Terms *83*
Allowable Charges *83*
Down Payment *84*
Eligibility Requirements *84*
VA FINANCING *85*
Purpose *85*
Veterans Eligible *85*
How to Apply *86*
Appraised Value *86*
Loan Guaranty *86*
Terms *87*
Loans *87*
Entitlement *88*
Occupancy Requirement *89*
Buyer Qualification *89*
Down Payment *89*
Closing Costs *90*
Points *90*
Impounds *90*
Trust Fund *90*
Prepayment Penalty *91*
VA—Mobile Homes *91*
ASSUMING & TAKING SUBJECT TO A MORTGAGE *93*
Assuming a Mortgage *93*
Taking Subject to a Mortgage *93*

ALL-INCLUSIVE TRUST DEED 95
Example of Effective Interest Yield on an AITD 96
Advantages to the Seller 96
Advantages to the Buyer 97
Precautionary Measures for Protection of the Seller 97
For the Protection of the Buyer 98
Points to Remember 98
FINANCING WITH NO MONEY DOWN 99
SECONDARY FINANCING 101
Sources for Secondary Financing 101
Market for Seconds 102
Terms of Notes 102
FINANCIAL DISCLOSURE—TRUTH IN LENDING ACT 103
Who It Applies To 104
Types of Credit Covered 104
Types of Credit Not Covered 104
Enforcement 105
Penalties 106
Annual Percentage Rate (APR) Defined 106
Finance Charge Defined 106
APR and Finance Charge Must be Clear 107
Regulation Z and Real Estate Loans 107
YIELD 109
LEVERAGE AND BORROWED MONEY 115
INDEX 117

THE MONEY SUPPLY AND INTEREST RATE

THE MONEY SUPPLY

Since the abandonment of gold as security for money in 1972, the value of money now lies primarily in the confidence of the people and the ability to exchange it for goods and services. In the past, other forms of value were used in trade, including precious metals, wampum, gems, and even salt. Today many primitive societies still continue to use such standards. Our modern world economy fluctuates on the tangible value of trust and confidence placed in those who rule our nations. When a country is strong, stable and productive, its currency is reflected by a high value compared to nations with low valued currencies who are floundering with political unrest and low productivity from continued changes.

Not only does the value of money continue to fluctuate, but the supply changes on a regular basis. The government agency responsible for the supply of money is the Federal Reserve Bank, often referred to as the "Fed," established by Congress in 1913. It is the central banker of the United States government and encompasses 12 branches plus 6,000-member commercial banks who are members of the system.

The actual decisions to either increase or decrease the money supply are made by 12 people who make up the Federal Open Market Committee. If the decision is to increase the money supply, it is implemented by a small number of dealers and large banks who are licensed to trade in government securities. The staff of the Federal Reserve will submit a check drawn on the Federal Reserve account to purchase government securities. The dealer delivers the securities and deposits the check in a bank. When the check is funded by the Federal Reserve, the bank will be credited with the additional funds composed of new currency printed by the Treasury. This addition of new funds into the economy will theoretically encourage more business activity.

Should the decision be to decrease the money supply, interest rates on Treasury Bills and the discount rate are increased causing the supply of lendable money to flow from savings accounts back into the Federal Reserve System, thereby taking funds out of circulation.

INTEREST RATES

Interest is the rate paid on an annual basis for the use of another's money. The rate of interest charged for borrowing depends on the overall supply of lendable funds and the risk associated with each particular loan. When the supply of money decreases, the rate of interest will increase.

The risk associated with a loan also has a bearing on the rate of interest charged to the borrower. Mortgage loans secured by real property offer one of the lowest rates of interest available. Conversely, loans made without security for the lender tend to carry the highest rates of interest. These rates charged by lenders fluctuate in the free market and are primarily influenced through the factors of supply and demand.

The Federal Reserve sets the discount rate which is the interest rate that member banks are charged by the Fed to borrow money. The federal government does not set maximum limits on interest rates charged by lenders, but state legislators do regulate maximum charges through usury laws.

In order to get a bearing on the direction interest rates are headed, various leading business magazines and newspapers publish certain interest rates daily that provide clues for real estate mortgage money.

The following are four interest rate indicators that can aid in determining this trend.

Treasury Bill Rate—Treasury Bills (T-Bills) are sold by the Federal Reserve Bank at weekly auctions and can be purchased from the bank or through authorized security dealers. T-Bills are sold at a minimum of $10,000 while interest rates on these bills are quoted on a weekly basis. The yield on this form of investment is expressed as a discount because it is the difference between the purchase price and the face value of the bill. For example, a $10,000, six-month T-Bill recently could be purchased for $9,527 returning a yield of 9.95%. At maturity, the return of $10,000 would yield $473 for six months' use of the money. The Treasury Bill rate is an excellent guide to reflecting the trend in the short term rate of money market funds.

Prime Rate—This is the most favorable interest rate charged by commercial banks to its best customers. The prime rate is often used as a base on which to set an entire class of loans. As an example, mortgage loans would be quoted to a borrower at one point over the prime rate, or construction loans at two points over prime. Most banks usually set their own prime lending rate, however, most will follow one of the leading commercial banks.

Federal Funds Rate—This is the rate of interest charged by one bank to another for money loaned on a short-term basis. When a bank's cash reserves fall below federal regulations due to prior loan commitments, it can call on another bank which may have a cash surplus and is willing to make a short-term loan. The interest rate charged varies from state to state, but the importance of this rate in relation to mortgage money is that the Fed watches it carefully in regulating the entire money supply. Should the federal funds rate increase over that of the previous week without the Fed adding money into the system to help reduce the rate, it is a true indication that the policy of the Fed is to tighten the money supply, all interest rates will eventually rise over the short term.

FNMA Auction Yield —This is the rate the *Federal National Mortgage Association* will buy home loans at over a four-month period. FNMA holds auctions every second Monday expressing an actual yield at which it will purchase home loans if the originator of the mortgages cannot get a better price elsewhere. The yield quoted is a consensus rate of what the participating lenders on that particular day would pay for mortgages over the next four months.

Lender expectations over the next four months for home loan rates tend to be reflected by the yields quoted. The following Tuesday after each auction, acceptance bids are published representing the purchase of large blocks of loans that will accurately indicate the future of home mortgage interest rates.

Besides these short term interest rate indicators, there is another which will have a long-term effect on future rates of interest charged for mortgage funds. Recently, the federal government passed new legislation allowing banks and savings and loans to increase saving deposit passbook rates. This increase in rates paid to depositors will have a long-term effect on mortgage money rates because lenders will now have to pay more for the funds they eventually loan out.

INTEREST

When $1000 is borrowed and $100 interest is charged, that represents a 10% annual rate of interest. The calculation of interest generally falls into three basic areas—simple, add-on, and compound. Since each technique is different, it is important to analyze each in detail.

SIMPLE INTEREST

This method is most commonly used on real estate loans. Interest is always calculated on the outstanding balance owed at the end of each payment period. Here are some sample problems to assist you in the mathematics involved.

Problem A – Simple note or loan of one year or less.

The formula is—

$$\frac{P \times R \times T}{360 \text{ (or } 365)} = i$$

This means the amount of money owed (P), times the annual interest rate (R), times the number of days you borrow the money (T), divided by 360 or 365. Financial institutions either use the 360-day year or the 365-day year, both are acceptable. Each is explained in greater detail later in the chapter.

$$\$1000 \times 5\% \text{ or } (.05) \times 90 \text{ (days)} \div 365 = \$12.33 \text{ interest.}$$

This method is the simplest form of interest computation, where no payments are made during the life of the loan. Only one final payment is made to repay the loan.

Problem B – Simple interest loans of more than one-year, often called interest-only loans.

Take for example a $10,000 loan at 10% interest for 3 years. Interest payments must be made at the end of each year. Here is how to calculate that annual interest payment.

$$\frac{\$10{,}000 \times 10\% \ (.10) \times 365}{365} = \$1000$$

or

$$\$10{,}000 \times 10\% \ (.10) = \$1000$$

After the first interest payment $10,000 is still owed, so the interest for the second year is still computed on the $10,000 loan. The interest will again be $1,000. At the end of the third year, while the interest is again $1,000, the entire amount borrowed will need to be repaid. That is, the final payment is $11,000.

Problem C – Simple interest loans where the borrower pays the interest at the end of each year, however, the borrower also repays a portion of the money owed.

Again using $10,000 loan at 10% interest for 3 years, the annual payment is $3,000 at the end of each year including principle and interest.

Here's how it works . . . At the end of the first year $3,000 is repaid. The interest portion is $1,000, as indicated in Problem B. The remaining $2,000 paid will reduce the amount of money owed to $8,000.

At the end of the second year another $3,000 is repaid. The interest portion is now calculated on the $8,000.

$$\$8{,}000 \times 10\% \ (.10) = \$800 \text{ interest}$$

Therefore, the $3,000 payment minus the $800 interest portion, reduces the amount of the loan by $2,200.

$$\$8{,}000 - \$2{,}200 = \$5{,}800 \text{ still owed}$$

At the end of the third and final year the interest is calculated on the $5,800.

$$\$5{,}800 \times 10\% = \$580 \text{ interest}$$

The remaining $5,800 on the loan plus the $580 interest must be repaid so the final payment is $6,380.

Simple interest loans are frequently amortized. An amortized loan has regular equal monthly payments which will pay off the entire loan completely at the end of the term, as opposed to having a balloon payment or balance owing at the end of the term.

For example, take a $5,000 loan at 9% interest for five years. As determined from a payment schedule book (to calculate by hand is next to impossible as a sophisticated computer is necessary to schedule a fully amortized loan), the monthly payment required to fully amortize this debt is $103.80. For the record the following sample schedule can be used as an example:

Original principal owing	$5,000.00
First month's interest calculated by $5,000 × 9% ÷ 12	37.50
Balance owing, end of first month	5,037.50
Monthly payment, determined by a payment schedule book	−103.80
Principal amount owing	4,933.70
Second month's interest, calculated by $4,933.70 × 9% ÷ 12	+37.00
Balance owing, end of second month	4,970.70
Monthly payment	−103.80
Principal amount owing	4,866.90

This schedule would continue for 60 months until the loan is paid in full.

The illustration on page 30 will graphically indicate how an amortized loan is completely paid off.

Amortized loans are normally available in various styles of payments including monthly, quarterly, semi-annual, and annual. Monthly loans are the most common. The reason is simple, the lender prefers to see regular payments being made by the borrower. It's difficult for a lender to wait one year for a payment, even if the borrower has excellent credit.

360 DAYS vs. 365 DAYS

Interest on a simple interest loan can be calculated either on a 360 or 365 day year. The difference is as follows.

360 Day Year

This assumes there are 12 equal 30-day months in the year. Therefore, if the interest rate is 12% and the payment scheme is monthly, simply divide the 12% (or .12) by 12 months.

$$12 \overline{) .12} \quad .01 = \text{monthly interest rate}$$

To determine the interest due each month, multiply .01 times the amount of money still owed.

$$\begin{array}{rl} \$10{,}000 & \text{owed} \\ \times .01 & \\ \hline \$100.00 & \text{interest for one month} \end{array}$$

If the payment scheme is quarterly, divide the annual rate by four; if semiannual divide the annual rate by two, and of course for annual payment follow example C.

365 Day Year (366 if Leap Year)

This calculation is similar in many ways, however one must arrive at a daily interest factor and then multiply that factor by the total actual days in the payment period.

If the annual interest rate is 10% and the payments are monthly, divide the annual interest rate by 365 (or 366 if Leap year).

$$365 \overline{) .10} \quad .00027397 = \text{daily interest factor}$$

Let's say the payment is for January, where there is 31 days. Multiply the amount of the loan balance owed times 31, then multiply the answer by .00027397.

$$\$10{,}000 \times 31 \times .00027397 = \$84.93 \text{ interest}$$

If compared to a 360 day calculation it would be as follows:

$$\frac{\$10{,}000 \times 10\%}{12} = \$83.33$$

There is $1.60 more interest in January on the 365-day calculation.

However in February the 83.33 (360 year plan) is the same, but the 365-day year interest is $76.71.

$$\$10{,}000 \times 28 \times .00027397 = \$76.71$$

That's $6.62 less interest on the 365 day year.

Don't let these different methods be misleading. While there will be differences each month, the total effect over a one-year period will be very similar with either the 360 or 365 method. Hand-calculate a schedule of interest charges for a whole year for each technique. You will find the results similar.

ODD DAYS INTEREST

This term refers to the interest that is charged on the beginning of the loan for the number of days over 30 to the first payment. If more days are allowed for the first payment, interest is charged for this period. It is frequently called *odd days interest* because the number of days will vary with each loan.

This is a reasonable cost that any lender will charge on a loan.

REMAINING BALANCE AND BALLOON PAYMENT

These terms apply to any real estate loan that is not amortized. That is, at the end of the loan, money is still owed. The amount of money owed is called the *remaining balance* or the *balloon payment.*

However, technically there is a difference. A balloon payment should include any accrued interest and a remaining balance only represents the amount of the loan still owed.

ADD-ON INTEREST

This type of interest is the exact opposite of simple. On a simple interest loan the interest is calculated on the amount of money still owed at the end of a payment period. In an add-on loan, the amount of interest is calculated at the beginning of the loan and is then spread over the term.

Example – $10,000 loan at 10% add-on interest; 12 months

$$\$10{,}000 \times .10 = \$1{,}000 \text{ interest}$$

This $1,000 is added-on to the loan (hence, the term add-on interest) amount to arrive at $11,000. To arrive at the monthly payment simply divide the $11,000 by 12 months.

$$12\overline{)\;1100.00\;}\quad = 91.666$$

To pay off the loan in a year 12 payments of $91.67 must be made. If repaying the loan early a portion of the interest is refunded in the form of a rebate called "The Rule of 78 Rebate." It's a complex formulae and far too difficult to explain here. However, it is sufficient to know the formulae is most beneficial to the lender and not the borrower.

This is not currently a popular type of loan. Congress is even attempting to outlaw its use, however, many lenders still use it.

COMPOUND INTEREST

Although this form of interest is not relevant to real estate loans, it is important to know exactly how it differs from other forms of interest.

At stated intervals during the life of an investment, the interest due is added to the principal and thereafter earns interest. The sum by which the original principal has increased at the end of the term of the investment is called the *compound interest.* The total amount due at the end of the term, which consists of the original principal plus the compound interest, is referred to as the *compound amount.*

An example of compound interest can be given when a person invests $10,000 in a savings account that earns 8% interest compounded quarterly. Since the quarterly interest rate would be one-fourth the annual rate we would first multiply the quarterly rate times the principal, then multiply the quarterly compound amount again times the quarterly rate, and continue this procedure until four quarters have elapsed. For example: $10,000 × .02 = $200, or the interest earned the first quarter. Now we add this to the original principal and multiply again by .02. $10,200 × .02 = $204, which is added to the first quarter's principal balance of $10,200, which equals $10,404. After continuing this process for the final two quarters, the result would be a compound amount of $10,824.32.

To compare compound with simple interest, at 8% simple interest the final amount earned by the depositor would be $800 ($10,000 × 8%), or $24.32 less than the interest earned with compound interest.

COMPARING ADD-ON TO SIMPLE INTEREST LOANS

In comparing the two forms of interest at a 10% annual rate

on a loan of $10,000 for a term of 15 years, the following results occur. With add-on interest the monthly payment including principal and interest to fully amortize the loan in 15 years is $138.88. The total finance charge on the $10,000 loan is $14,998 with an annual percentage rate (APR) of 14.84%.

Under the same conditions with a similar simple interest loan, the monthly payment is $107.47 including principal and interest. The total finance charge is $9,345 with an annual percentage rate of 10%.

	Finance Charge	Monthly Payment	APR
Add-on	$14,998	$138.88	14.84%
Simple	$ 9,345	$107.47	10%

It is obvious from the above chart that there are substantial savings rendered under a simple interest loan, as opposed to an add-on interest loan. The key to the consumer is to check the APR. That will give a better indication of the cost of money in most instances.

This large difference between the add-on and simple interest rate is the primary reason for the *Regulation Z – Truth in Lending* law of 1969. This required lenders to indicate the APR on all consumer loans. Prior to 1969 there was no real way to compare the interest cost on a loan.

AMORTIZED LOAN

A loan in which the principal payments are paid in installments, **AND IS COMPLETELY PAID OFF!**

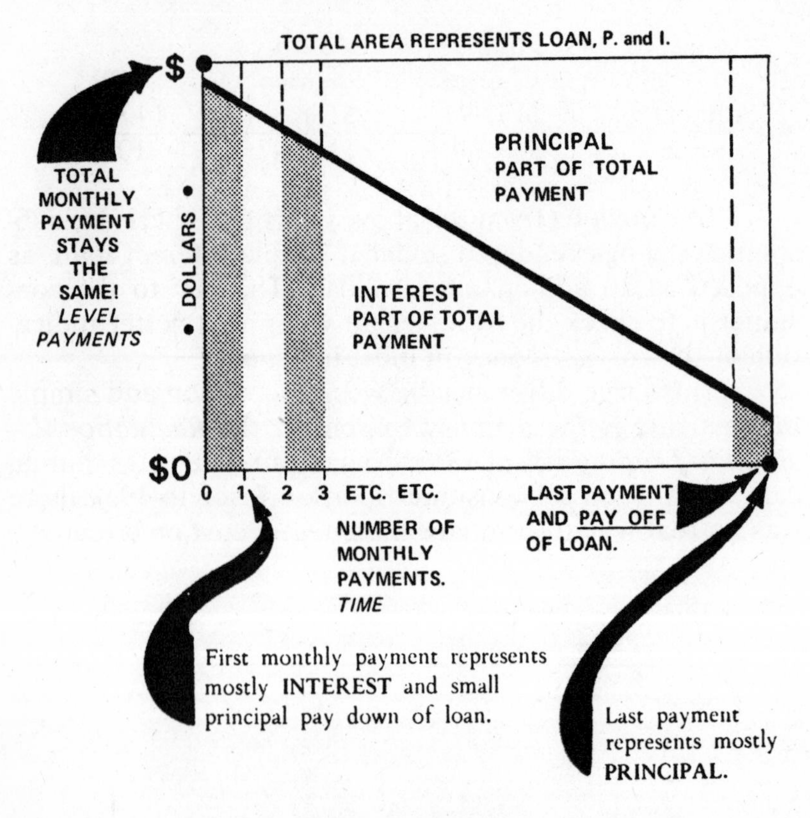

Reprinted from 'INCOME PROPERTY ILLUSTRATED'
By Roy T. Maloney

SOURCES OF REAL ESTATE FINANCING

Although commercial banks rank the largest with respect to overall volume of lending for the short and long term business, commercial, and mortgage loans, savings and loan associations supply the largest percentage of real estate financing.

The function of mortgage lenders has been essentially the same over the centuries. Starting in the early days of America, countrymen who were fortunate enough to save any money joined with others to pool their funds in a safe place. These accumulated savings would then be loaned to other members of the community to build or improve their property.

SAVINGS AND LOAN ASSOCIATIONS

Since those early colonial days, a lot has happened to improve these thrift institutions. Before the Great Depression there was little government regulation to watch over these associations, but the Depression brought to the surface the many inherent problems which before were not evident.

The major problem was flexibility due to the long term nature of the majority of their lending. This often caused liquidity problems when depositors suddenly decided to withdraw needed funds. The crisis was overcome in 1932 by the creation of the *Federal Home Loan Bank Board.* This authority, which is still in operation today, provided member associations with liquidity by offering a continuing source of funds for emergencies or additional mortgage loans.

Then in 1933, the Federal Home Loan Bank Board was given the authorization to issue federal charters to newly formed savings and loans. These charters regulated methods of operation and required certain standards of compliance. In 1934, the *Federal Savings and Loan Insurance Corporation* (FSLIC) was created to provide insurance on deposits for all federally chartered associations. That insurance coverage currently protects any one depositor up to $40,000.

Although the Federal Home Loan Bank Board governs federally chartered savings and loan associations, there are also state chartered associations. The majority of the financing made available by these thrift institutions is in the form of conventional loans secured by residential real estate and sometimes commercial property. They also underwrite VA and FHA loans which are considered to be non-conventional loans. In addition, they make loans for construction, home improvement and on mobile homes. They are not authorized to make consumer or business loans.

MUTUAL SAVINGS BANKS

Their origins are similar to that of savings and loans, they exist primarily in the Northeastern and Northwestern areas of the United States. They are all state chartered and mutually owned by their depositors, although managed by an elected group of trustees.

Their investment portfolio consists of approximately 75% mortgage loans, and the balance is made up of government securities, personal and consumer type loans.

COMMERCIAL BANKS

Commercial banks are the largest of all lenders, but only 12% of their investment portfolio is in the form of mortgage loans. The bulk of their financing involves business and consumer loans. Larger banks are an important source of commercial and industrial real estate financing. And can either be state or federally chartered.

State chartered banks must comply to the regulations of a state banking board or commission while national banks are under the jurisdiction of the *Federal Reserve System.* The *Federal Deposit Insurance Corporation* (FDIC) insures the deposits of its members up to $40,000. State banks can also belong to the FDIC, but must comply with state regulations.

INSURANCE COMPANIES

Insurance companies were not initially created for the purpose of providing long term real estate financing. Their primary interest is to supply a high yield on investment funds, yet at a low risk to provide safety for policy holder's money which is available on mortgages secured by real property.

They are governed by the state in which they operate. The bulk of their lending is long term and usually on large income producing real estate including residential, commercial as well as industrial. Often they will require equity participation when large real estate projects are to be financed.

CREDIT UNIONS

The employees of many companies have formed credit unions for the benefit of their own members. They are an invaluable source of funds and credit unions pay their depositors interest on savings, and have year end profit sharing. The majority of their lendable funds are loaned to members for the purchase of cars and furniture. Recently, some have started making long term real estate loans at very reasonable interest rates.

PRIVATE MORTGAGE INSURANCE

Numerous private mortgage insurance companies are now insuring real estate loans similar to that of FHA. A portion of the loan is insured against default by the borrower, which is paid for by a premium charged to the borrower.

Private mortgage insurance allows lenders to make higher loan-to-value ratios, thereby allowing more buyers to purchase with less of a down payment. Furthermore, discounts or points are eliminated due to the fact that interest rates are the effective rates in the prevailing money market.

MORTGAGE BANKERS

Mortgage bankers function as a financial intermediary between institutional lenders and borrowers bringing both together for a fee. This fee, or commission is usually one to two percent of the funds appropriated. They do not fund the money directly, but appropriate the money then administer and service the loan for a fee. This additional service fee usually falls within a range of one half to one percent of the loan proceeds, depending on the extent of the service provided. They usually represent insurance companies, savings and loan associations, and pension funds.

MORTGAGE COMPANIES

Mortgage companies operate similar to mortgage bankers only they represent private lenders and government backed loans, such as VA and FHA loans.

HOME LOAN COMPANIES

Home loan companies also operate similarly to the above financial intermediaries, except they deal mostly in second trust deeds and represent private investors. Their fee for originating and servicing the loan is between 10 and 20 points which is charged to the borrower.

LOAN BROKERS

Loan brokers function as a financial intermediary, however they can represent lenders directly or they can represent any of the above three types of companies.

Organized solutions to the variety of problems related to real estate financing would not exist today without the presence of loan brokers. They bring the borrower and lender together and monitor the many legal safeguards and other controls available to assure the security of the transaction. To fulfill their obligation, they must not only protect the individual lender, but the borrower as well.

Licensed real estate brokers are authorized to act as loan brokers in many states. In practice, some real estate brokers arrange loans, and others sell property; the two tend to specialize. The loan broker arranges financing through private lenders for prospective home buyers who do not have sufficient funds to make up the difference between a first mortgage and the total sales price. The loan broker serves the real estate salesman as a clearing house of available loans, freeing him to concentrate on his basic objective . . . sales.

Loan brokers serve the borrower by arranging funds for specific needs that might otherwise not be available. One such instance would be when a prospective home buyer does not have the difference between the first mortgage and the total sales price. Another would be when a homeowner requires funds for an emergency but doesn't have adequate credit or collateral except for his home. In either event, the loan broker could arrange for secondary financing through a private lender.

Loan broker services are not restricted to arranging first and second loans through private lenders. They usually represent most institutional lenders, plus union, private pension and trust funds, and surplus corporate funds. A first mortgage or trust deed may be financed through an institutional lender with the broker negotiating the most favorable loan possible on behalf of the borrower.

If time is of the essence, the broker may advise arranging a second mortgage through a private lender. When the broker receives and approves an application for such a loan, he seeks out a lender usually from a list of contacts.

At this time, the role of the loan broker as an intermediary between two laymen becomes particularly important. As a professional with knowledge of economic trends and real estate values, he advises how much may be safely borrowed, arranges title searches and escrow services, provides title and fire insurance, and secures all other safeguards.

It is also the responsibility of the loan broker to protect the borrower against illegal charges. Real estate loan brokers provide their borrowers with a full disclosure of finance and interest charges. These disclosures are in writing and outline all charges such as the annual interest, broker's loan fee, and all escrow fees. Upon completion of the transaction, a borrower knows exactly the proceeds of the loan as well as the charges.

Serving the lender, whether private or institutional, the real estate loan broker has generated a large volume of business. This generation of second mortgages and trust deeds has made possible the purchase of homes by hundreds of thousands of families who otherwise could not afford them. This has increased the demand for first trust deeds and mortgages, contributing to an increase in overall mortgage activity and to an expansion of the overall economy.

The loan broker, along with his fellow real estate brokers, is closer to the broad source of demand for financing then a specific institution. He acts informally as a "field man" to generate this additional volume.

To the private lender the loan broker has become a source of sound real estate investment opportunities yielding a fair rate of return. These investments have the advantage of being secured by real property that has been appraised by experienced people. They usually are short term, provide reasonable liquidity, and yield an annual rate of return of 10% to 12% interest.

Brokers not only serve lenders as a medium of investment, but provide a number of services for their protection. They investigate and appraise the property involved, create and record the loan documents, and set up the mechanics for making the transaction convenient. At the option of the lender, they may assist in making collections.

Investing through a loan broker provides the lender with unusual flexibility. He may choose a first mortgage or trust deed, offering longer term stability at a lesser rate of interest. Or he may choose a second mortgage or trust deed for higher interest over a shorter period.

Should the holder of a mortgage or trust deed find it impractical to hold it to maturity, he may sell it at a discount, either to a broker or to a private investor through a broker. In some circumstances the broker may advise the owner of a note to keep it and borrow with the note as collateral. When he borrows on the note immediate cash is realized as it would if he had sold it, but ownership is still retained. The privilege of realizing most of the principal and the balance of the interest is still available.

Thus the real estate loan broker not only helps arrange the investment, but also is in a position to assist with any problems that may arise out of an unforseen need for liquidity.

EXISTING SELLERS

Often sellers of real property will carry the necessary financing to accommodate the purchase of property. This is most often the case during tight money conditions within our economy; or when the seller doesn't need the equity out of the property being sold and he wishes a continuing return on his money without reinvesting it.

This is a most efficient method of financing. By avoiding institutional lenders, one can save numerous costly fees which are often associated with these lenders. In addition, the buyer can usually negotiate with the seller for a reasonable rate of interest which can have a profound effect on savings over the term of the loan.

FUNCTIONING OF THE MONEY MARKET

Lending institutions take in deposits from the public and

pay interest. These deposits are then loaned out, or invested in various ways. Profit is earned on the spread in interest rates paid to depositors and the interest earned on outstanding loans and investments. For example, savings and loans pay interest on deposits from 5.5% to 8%, depending on the term (savings accounts). These deposits are then loaned out for real estate loans, etc. The gross profit is the difference in the rates they are earning and the rate they are paying to depositors. Usually, a bank or savings and loan can break even with an 0.5% differential in spread; anything over the 0.5% spread is profit.

Two other institutions in the money market are the *Federal National Mortgage Association*, nicknamed "Fanny Mae," and the *Government National Mortgage Association*, known as "Ginny Mae." These two organizations add liquidity (cash flow) to the entire financial industry by purchasing seasoned mortgages at discounted rates from lending institutions.

For example, a bank or savings and loan, which lacks ample cash to make more loans, can sell existing mortgages at discounted rates to one of these secondary money market institutions and loan the proceeds out again at the going market rate. Both associations can buy an existing 9% mortgage for about 8.5% (discounted) and earn the 0.5% differential as profit. The loans they purchase must be *seasoned*, which means prompt payments have been made by the borrower for an extended period of time, thereby representing a good payment record. Usually, a lending institution will present a package of loans to the secondary market, rather than individually.

HOW TO BORROW MONEY

Institutional lenders do not loan money on the basis of need but rather on the ability of the borrower to repay the loan.

The following material covered on this topic are basic principles to guide you when it's time to borrow money.

1. Update your credit, if it isn't current.

2. Complete financial requirements of money needed, and how it will be paid back are required before you make the loan request.

3. Prepare an accurate financial statement.

4. To gain the maximum return on investment always borrow the highest repayable amount, with the lowest possible payments for the longest period of time. Don't borrow more than can be safely repaid.

5. When applying for a loan, have exact figures prepared. If a home improvement loan is required for $5,000, a complete breakdown of what the improvements will be and how much they will cost should be completed.

When this data is prepared, it's time to make a loan request. A good presentation can determine the ultimate success as requests will require some salesmanship. The idea is really to sell the lender on loaning the money.

All paperwork should be legible and organized, showing a complete picture of proposed financial plans. Personally contact the lender, and be dressed in businesslike attire. Be confident, and get to the point. The lender wants to know what the loan is for and how it will be paid back. After all questions the lender has are answered a loan application must be completed. Once an agreement is reached, the borrower will be notified at a later date if the loan is approved.

Convince the lender that the proposed plans are sound and that repaying the loan is the main objective. Lenders are anxious to loan money, that's their business.

SHOULD YOU REFINANCE OR TAKE OUT A SECOND LOAN?

At some point in time after owning a home for a number of years one might consider purchasing a second property as an investment. The question is, assuming there is still a substantial amount owed on the first mortgage, should a person refinance the existing home or take out a second loan against it? In most cases, the existing mortgage will be at an interest rate far below the current market interest rate for new home mortgage loans. If this holds true, then it would be unwise to refinance because that would be eliminating the value of the existing low interest loan by replacing it with a costlier high interest rate loan.

Take for example a home purchased five years ago for $50,000 with a $40,000 mortgage attached at 8% interest for a term of 30 years. The principal and interest payment would be approximately $300 a month. The remaining principal balance owing after five years would be about $38,000. Assume further that the current market value of the home is worth $80,000. Therefore, there is $42,000 equity in the home ($80,000 − $38,000 = $42,000).

If the home is refinanced at an 11.5% rate of interest, the lender would advance a maximum of 80% of the market value, of which $38,000 must be applied toward paying off the balance on the original loan. Thus, there would be $26,000 in net proceeds ($80,000 × 80% = $64,000 − $38,000 = $26,000). The new first mortgage would require monthly payments of $634 to amortize principal and interest over the term of 30 years.

If a second mortgage is arranged for an amount equal to that of refinancing which is $26,000, the lender would charge about two percentage points higher in rate of interest for a maximum term of 15 years. Therefore, on a loan of $26,000 for 15 years at a 13.5% interest rate, the monthly payment would be about $338. Total monthly payments for the next 15 years including the existing payment on the first mortgage would be $638 ($338 + $300). After 15 years the second mortgage would be fully paid which then would only require a monthly payment on the first mortgage of $300 per month.

REFINANCE

Amount of net proceeds	Payment on 1st	Term of loan	Total amount Paid over term of loan
$26,000	$634	30 yrs	$228,240

TAKING A SECOND MORTGAGE

Amount of net proceeds	Payment on 1st	Term remaining on 1st	Payment on 2nd	Term remaining on 2nd	Total paid over term of loan
$26,000	$300	25 yrs	$338	15 yrs	$150,840

From the above example, the difference in amounts paid over the full term of the loan is a savings of $77,400 by taking out a second mortgage as opposed to refinancing. There are two basic reasons for the huge differential in these two methods of financing. First, when the property is refinanced at the higher interest rate of 11.5% then 3.5 percentage points have been added to a 30 year loan, of which over half of the proceeds went to pay off $38,000 on the original principal amount. The second reason is that although a 13.5% second mortgage appears at first to be a high rate of interest, it is only for a term of 15 years.

During the life of an amortized loan, the initial payments are mostly interest. As time goes on, the interest paid becomes a smaller portion of the payment, and more of the payment goes toward equity build up.

The only time one could possibly consider refinancing a home over taking a second mortgage would be when prevailing market interest rates for mortgages are below that rate which a person is already paying on the existing first mortgage.

FINANCIAL INSTRUMENTS AND LOANS

There are many types of financial instruments, however, most real estate financing derived from banks and savings and loans are in two basic forms: mortgages and trust deeds. It is important to understand the other common loan types, not only for real estate but also because additional financing may be required for other purposes.

FINANCIAL INSTRUMENTS

Mortgages – A mortgage or deed of trust from a lender is referred to as conventional financing when VA and FHA government backed loans are *not* involved. Both are agreements between borrower and lender creating liens against real estate. In other words, the agreement states that, should the borrower default on the loan (fail to make payments when due), mortgages and trust deeds will allow the lender to sell the property in order to satisfy the loan obligation.

The two parties involved in a mortgage are referred to as the *mortgagor*, who is the property owner or borrower, and the *mortgagee*, or lender. There are two parts to a mortgage: the *Mortgage Note*, which is evidence of the debt; and the *Mortgage Contract*, which is security for the debt. The note promises to repay the loan, while the contract promises to convey title of the property to the mortgagee in case of default.

There has been a recent trend towards *variable rate mortgages*, which allow the lender to raise or lower interest rates during the term of a conventional loan. The use of this option by the lender will depend upon the fluctuations in the money market. The amount of increase or decrease is regulated.

During periods of high inflation a fixed rate of interest is very advantageous to the borrower because he pays back the loan with deflated dollars. During periods of deflation, the variable rate mortgage would be advantageous to the borrower. However, a condition of deflation is very unlikely to occur in our economy. Even if it did, it would most likely only occur for a very short time.

OPEN-END MORTGAGES

This form of security instrument permits a lender to advance additional funding under the same priority and security as the original mortgage. It is typically used in farm loans where the lender maintains a continuing relationship with the borrower, and because of the need of the borrower to be continually making additions to the farm. As the borrower progressively pays the principal balance down, he may wish to improve the farm with a new corral or silo. The additional funds can easily be arranged under the terms of an open-end mortgage.

The advantage of this form of financing to the farmer-rancher borrower is evident in the lack of further delays in arranging a new loan, avoiding the expense and inconvenience of title searches and recording a new mortgage.

CONSTRUCTION MORTGAGES

A construction loan, also referred to as *interim financing*, is used to build a new house or other type of facility. This type of mortgage is similar in security to a first mortgage on real property; but the proceeds of the loan are disbursed to the developer as the building is being constructed. Here the borrower is allowed to draw a portion of the funds at various stages of construction as work is completed.

Due to the high risk associated with construction financing, high interest rates are usually prevalent with funding for a short term, usually up to three years. Often, before construction financing is committed to the builder, the lender will require that permanent financing or a *take-out commitment* be assured by a reputable lender once the project is completed.

Builders create individual homes and large developed tracts which are eventually sold speculatively to consumers. The lender must look forward to the actual sale of an individual home to pay off the construction loan. This increases the risk to the lender which is the reason he may require the developer to obtain a *stand-by* permanent loan commitment before construction begins.

MORTGAGES WITH RELEASE CLAUSES

Under conventional mortgages, there is no provision allowing the partial sale of a property, as in the development of a large tract of homes where individual improved lots are sold. In this case it is necessary to have specific release procedures enabling the developer to sell lots, or a portion of the land, and deliver clear title to that portion. The provisions in this form of mortgage state that the developer can pay off a portion of the loan as each lot is sold and obtain a release of that portion from the original mortgage. In a subdivision where individual lots are to be sold, the developer is usually required by the lender to pay a percentage of the sales price of the lot for each lot released. The entire mortgage obligation would be amortized so that about 60% to 80% of the lots would fully amortize the entire loan obligation.

Trust Deeds – are similar to mortgages except that an additional third party is involved, and the foreclosure period is shorter.

With a trust deed, the property owner or borrower is called the *trustor,* and the lender is the *beneficiary.* The intermediate party, whose job it is to hold title to the property for the security of the lender, is called the *trustee.*

Should the trustor default on his loan obligation, the subject property will be sold by the trustee at public auction through a *power of sale* clause contained in all trust deeds, without court procedure.

FORECLOSURE

The foreclosure process is quite lengthy and complex and procedures vary by statutes of each state according to the location of the property. Essentially, foreclosure is the procedure the lender takes to redeem his interest in a property through public auction of the subject property should the borrower default on his loan obligation.

In case of mortgages, should the mortgagor default,

the property can then be sold through foreclosure in a court action. First, the mortgagee must obtain a foreclosure judgement from the court, which orders the sheriff to sell the property to the highest bidder (over and above what is due to the lender). The property is then put up for public auction. Should a successful bid be made, the bidder receives a document known as the *Certificate of Sale* from the sheriff. The bidder must then hold the certificate for one year before he will be issued the deed to the property. If the mortgagor pays the bidder sufficient monies within that year (bid price plus interest), the mortgagor then retains ownership of the property and the foreclosure sale is nullified.

The period during which a mortgagor is entitled to redeem his property is referred to as the mortgagors's *Equity of Redemption.*

In the case of trust deeds, foreclosure is initiated by a *Notice of Default,* which is recorded by the trustee, with a copy sent to the trustor. After three months, a *Notice of Sale* is posted on the property, and an advertisement for sale is carried in local newspapers once a week for three weeks.

During this period, if the trustor fails to pay the beneficiary sufficient funds to halt the foreclosure (overdue loan payments, plus interest, penalties and fees), the sale will then be conducted by the trustee.

Proceeds from foreclosure are disbursed to the beneficiary, then to any other lien holders.

Second Mortgages and Trust Deeds – An owner of real estate is entitled to arrange more than one loan against the same property, which then stands as security against default for the payment of the second loan. This "junior" or "subordinate" loan is called a *second* because it is second in priority to a first loan with respect to a claim upon the proceeds from foreclosure.

During the course of many real estate transactions, secondary financing becomes necessary in order to consummate the transaction when conventional financing, along with the down payment, may be insufficient to accommodate the purchase price. If the savings and loan institution will lend only 80% of the purchase price, and the buyer can only put up a 10% down payment, the balance of 10% can be obtained through such additional financing. Often, a secondary loan is carried by the seller in the form of a second mortgage or trust deed.

Occasionally, more than two loans may be involved with a particular property, and the risk to the borrower is no greater with one loan or with ten, providing he can make the payments.

While each income-producing property is a business in its own right, income left to spend, expenses and debt service are important factors in a sale. It is important to negotiate with the seller for ideal financing in order to attain the highest investment return.

Most secondary financing involves a term of three to five years, and carries interest rates slightly higher than first mortgages and trust deeds. Monthly payments are typically one percent of the amount financed (i.e., a secondary loan for $10,000 will have monthly payments of $100). Secondary financing can be structured to the buyer's advantage through reduction of monthly payments and/or an increase in the term of the loan beyond the normal five years.

In today's market, with skyrocketing inflation and escalating real estate values, it is to the borrower's advantage to secure long-term loans. The dollars you borrow at today's values are paid back, because of inflation, at tomorrow's lesser deflated values.

Naturally, you continue to pay interest on indebtedness—but you will continue to prosper if you do so, because your appreciation is so much greater than the cost of indebtedness.

LAND CONTRACT

Also referred to as a *Conditional Sales Contract* or *Contract of Sale.* This form of agreement is strictly a contract between buyer and seller, without a financial intermediary involved. The buyer agrees to purchase a property and pays principal and interest to the seller along with a down payment. The title to the property remains vested with the seller until the conditions of the contract are fulfilled. The buyer retains possession to the property but should he default on the agreement, the property reverts back to the seller.

This form of financing real estate is ideal during "tight money" conditions as interest rates on a Land Contract can be set between buyer and seller, often at lesser rates than current market rates. Furthermore, a more lenient down payment may be required by the seller or less restrictive credit requirements can be offered because no financial intermediary is involved in this form of transaction.

It is important to understand that a Land Contract is in fact a security device, similar to that of a mortgage or deed of trust, but differs in the respect that there is no standard form and some of the legal remedies are not clearly defined.

It is also important that the Land Contract be recorded similar to a mortgage or deed of trust and title insurance in favor of the buyer be required.

VA Loans – This is a government backed loan extended to veterans, entitling them to borrow money for homes, mobile homes, and farms with 100% financing at low interest rates. The VA loan is underwritten and processed by conventional lenders, but a portion is guaranteed by the Veteran's Administration against default.

In order to protect the veteran himself and assist the lender in approving the loan, the Veteran's Administration will have the property appraised and will issue a *Certificate of Reasonable Value* (CRV). A veteran may purchase a home at whatever price he wishes to pay but a VA loan cannot be secured for more than the CRV. Any amount in excess of that must be paid in cash by the veteran.

Although a portion of the loan is guaranteed by the VA, the veteran must repay the lender and, if he defaults, will lose his property. Any loss incurred by the lender will be compensated by the VA, but the veteran must eventually repay the government.

FHA Loans—These government-backed loans, under the supervision of the *Federal Housing Administration* (FHA), are not restricted to veterans but are also available to other individuals who meet the requirements of the FHA. An FHA loan is underwritten and processed by conventional lending institutions, and the lender is similarly insured against default by the buyer. Thus, the lender is able to grant longer and more lenient terms, so that FHA loans offer a lower interest rate and smaller down payment than conventional financing. The subject of VA and FHA financing will be detailed in later chapters.

VA & FHA Loan Assumption—Many properties on the market today are available with existing VA and FHA loans attached, whereas the seller initiated a new VA or FHA loan when he purchased the property and now he wishes to sell. These properties are by far the best bargains because they offer the following advantages: No credit qualification by the buyer, which saves time and up to $100 in credit application fees. No loan origination fee, which is usually 1% of the loan being made; however, there is usually a nominal $35 assumption fee charged to the buyer. The last and greatest advantage is that the buyer assumes the existing rate of interest for the entire term of the loan, a rate which is usually substantially lower than prevailing interest rates.

Points and Fees—When a lending institution has been collecting for some time on a particular mortgage, and the payments have been regularly made, the loan is called a *seasoned* loan, meaning that it represents an outstanding credit situation.

When an FHA or VA loan is seasoned, the lending institution may decide to sell it for less than the remaining principal amount, in order to receive cash which then can be lent out at a higher rate of interest. It is to their advantage to do this because of the low interest rates fixed by the Federal Government on guaranteed loans. The loan is discounted because otherwise, with the low interest rates, it would be difficult to attract buyers. (A loan may also be sold without a discount, of course. It is to the lender's advantage to sell a loan if he can then lend the monies out at a higher rate.)

The mortgage market is a critical part of the economy, and the low interest rates of government-backed loans might not attract investors as they seek higher yields elsewhere, unless the discount points are used to make the mortgage loan attractive to an investor.

A *discount point* represents 1/8% additional yield on a mortgage. Thus, if an FHA or VA loan at 8 1/2% is discounted 4 points or 1/2% (4 x 1/8%), this means that the loan is sold by the mortgagee to an investor for an amount which will enable the investor to earn 9% on his money. The owner/buyer then makes his payments, the same as before, to the new holder of the mortgage.

Loan fees—These charges to the buyer cover the lender's expenses. These expenses include credit investigations, loan application evaluation, and appraisal of the subject property.

ACCELERATION CLAUSE

This refers to a stipulation in a note of debt obligation requiring immediate payment in full of the unpaid balance upon the occurrence of a specified event.

The *due-on-sale clause* is another form of acceleration. It states that at the choice of the lender, the entire balance is due immediately upon the transfer, sale or extended encumbrance of the property.

Although an acceleration clause is optional, a lender cannot accelerate the liability without it.

The lender can, with respect to the due-on-sale clause, exercise or renege the option to accelerate. Should a buyer desire to assume a loan, the lender can either approve or disapprove the assumption. If approved, the lender can charge an assumption fee or an increase in interest rate if the existing loan can be demanded.

PREPAYMENT

In most long term real estate loans, the borrower cannot repay a loan before maturity unless the lender consents, or unless the terms of the note expressly permit it by stating periodic payments of a specific sum or more. Most lenders usually charge a *prepayment penalty* or fee, if the loan is paid off before maturity. This fee is often equal to six months' interest on the loan.

OTHER TYPES OF LOANS

The following describes the various types of loans that are available to you as an investor for purposes other than the actual purchase of real property.

Chattel Loans are mortgages which are secured by personal, rather than real, property. Automobiles, furniture, boats and business equipment normally qualify for security against a chattel loan. These loans are short-term, and the interest rate may be as much as double that of conventional real estate loans.

Commercial Loans are the best source of short-term money and usually require a signature only. Such loans can be obtained only if your credit and financial statement are such that you are considered to be, personally, a good risk. These loans are best used for seasonal expenses and large purchases (for example, taxes, or equipment that is on sale). Commercial loan interest rates are slightly higher than conventional real estate loans.

Personal Loans, unlike commercial loans, are made for non-business uses, and are usually paid back in installments. Credit unions and finance companies use this type of loan, with interest rates charged on the unpaid balance. The rates for personal loans vary from 12% to 18%.

Home Improvement Loans can be obtained for the purpose of remodeling, repairs and additions to real property. Terms vary up to five years, with regular monthly payments on installment being the standard form, although other forms are also available, such as the FHA Title I Home Improvement Loan. Interest rates are higher than for conventional real estate, but are still favorable, such that home improvement loans are usually excellent sources of financing.

LOAN COMMITMENTS

In order for loan brokers, builders, and other various individuals who depend on mortgage funds to operate efficiently, it is necessary that certain types of promises or loan commitments by lenders be made for available funds. The procedures and terminology may vary throughout the country but the intention of each form of commitment tends to be rather uniform. The following categories describe such loan commitments.

FUTURE COMMITMENT

This form of commitment is used in pledging funds for a building yet to be constructed. It may include terminology such as "on or before September 30, 1980"; or it might encompass a time span such as "this loan commitment cannot be exercised before 12 months nor later than 24 months from date of this agreement."

Future commitment is a pledge of a certain specified amount of money that is made available at a later specific date.

Actual use of the money funded under a future commitment does not have to be mandatory. But if the holder of the commitment finds a cheaper source of funding elsewhere, the commitment fee is forfeited.

The lender usually charges the holder of this form of commitment a fee; a total of one to two percentage points of the funds promised, but the fee is negotiable. Lenders feel that a fee is necessary in pledging funds at fixed interest rates at some future date. Perhaps rightly so as interest rates have fluctuated so much in the past.

FORWARD LOAN COMMITMENT

This form of commitment is usually between a lender and mortgage company which also spells out the type of loan and conditions the lender will accept. In addition, it describes the services provided by the mortgage company and the fees charged for such services.

Under this form of commitment, a specific amount of money is available for certain types of loans at a fixed rate of interest. The mortgage company is authorized to a service charge of one-tenth to one-half of one percent of the loan for providing loan escrow services, handling collections and paying taxes and insurance. Usually the term of this commitment set by the lender does not extend beyond six months.

The commitment fee, if required, is usually one percent of the funds committed and is due at the time of issuance of the commitment. Normally the commitment fee is refundable when the pledge is 100% utilized. Should the entire commitment not be fully used, the mortgage company might be required to forfeit a portion of the fee.

TAKE-OUT COMMITMENTS

This form of money pledge, also referred to as a *stand-by* commitment, is used on any kind of proposed construction. It is a commitment that is actually a back-up promise because it really is never intended to be used but is available if needed. It is most often used during tight money conditions and is issued at an interest rate higher than the prevailing market rate. Usually the developer will have three to five years to exercise his option to use the commitment at a cost of two to four points.

The true purpose of a take-out commitment is to assure the developer of construction financing, just in case funding is not available through a construction loan. The developer would forfeit the commitment fee if he were to obtain a more reasonable permanent loan.

PERMANENT LOAN COMMITMENT

This is the final mortgage loan which is amortized over a term of up to 40 years. On a single family residence, a permanent loan is actually made to the buyer as an immediate commitment, or a future commitment made prior to construction of the house.

Before a commercial development can begin, a permanent loan or a valid take-out commitment must be assured before a construction loan can be funded.

FEDERAL HOUSING ADMINISTRATION (FHA) FINANCING

The FHA insures loans made by approved financial institutions, generally savings and loans associations, commercial banks and insurance companies, and mortgage loan brokers.

FHA PROGRAMS COVERED

TITLE II-Sec. 203(b) – Finance the acquisition of one to four family dwellings, either proposed, under construction, or existing.

TITLE II-Sec. 203(b) – Veterans

TITLE II-Sec. 207 – Finance the acquisition of mobile home parks and rental housing.

TITLE II-Sec. 221(d)(2) – Finance the acquisition of existing or proposed, or rehabilitation of low cost one to four family dwellings for displaced families, or one family homes for low or moderate income families.

TITLE II-Sec. 221 (d) (4) – Finance the rehabilitation or construction of five or more dwelling units.

TITLE II-Sec. 222 – Finance the acquisition of owner-occupied homes for service personnel.

TITLE II-Sec. 223(f) – Finance the acquisition or the refinancing of existing multi-family dwellings.

TITLE II-Sec. 234(c) – Finance the acquisition of individually owned condominium units.

TITLE II-Sec. 234(d) – Finance the acquisition of condominiums and projects that will be converted to condos upon completion.

TITLE II-Sec. 235 – To aid lower income families by paying part of the family's mortgage interest payment on low cost homes, duplexes or condos.

FHA Sec. 245 – Graduated Payment Mortgage (GPM).

TITLE I-Mobile Homes – Finance the acquisition of mobile homes which must be used by the owner as his principal residence.

FHA TITLE II-Sec. 203(b) – ONE TO FOUR FAMILY DWELLINGS

PURPOSE

It is the purpose of this FHA program to offer guaranteed financing to lenders to accommodate the purchase of proposed, under construction, or existing one to four family dwellings.

QUALIFYING

While the FHA does not recommend a specific practice, the following ratio can be used to determine the buyer's chances to qualify for an FHA loan. The gross monthly liabilities need to be four times the monthly payment (which includes principal and interest, FHA Mutual Mortgage Insurance, hazard insurance, and real estate taxes).

The gross monthly income consists of: applicant's base salary, overtime pay (if verified and likely to continue), spouse's income, net income from rental property, and co-signers or co-mortgagors (if they have a continuing interest in the property and mortgagor).

LOAN TERMS

Maximum loan of $90,000 on one-family dwellings.

Maximum loan of $101,300 on two-family dwellings.

Maximum loan of $122,600 on three-family dwellings.

Maximum loan of $142,600 on four-family dwellings.

The maximum number of units that will qualify for an FHA loan under Title II-Sec. 203(b) is four.

The maximum FHA loan may not exceed 85% of the above loans when it is to non-resident owners.

The maximum term is 30 years or 75% of the existing economic life of the property, whichever is less. If the buyer does not qualify at a term of 30 years, it may be increased to 35 years.

Interest rates are adjusted by the FHA Commissioner as necessary.

MORTGAGE INSURANCE

The FHA charges the borrower a 1/2% per annum premium on the average outstanding loan balance to insure the lender against loss. This charge decreases slightly each year over the life of the loan.

PERCENTAGE OF LOAN TO VALUE

The maximum loan equals 97% on the first $25,000 and 95% on the excess.

Maximum loan of 90% of appraised value and closing costs is permitted when property is less than one year old, and not built under HUD/FHA inspections.

DOWN PAYMENT

The down payment on new FHA loans must be in the form of cash or other assets including existing mortgage or deeds of trust.

It is prohibited to attain secondary financing for the down payment. The only exception is when a buyer is 62 years of age or older. A person in this situation may borrow the down payment and closing costs from a person or corporation approved by the FHA but not a broker or lending institution. The buyer must still meet the qualifications for monthly payments of the supplementary loan.

CLOSING COSTS – PERMITTED TO BUYER

Item	Maximum Closing Costs
1. FHA Application Fee	$65.00 on proposed and $50.00 on existing.
2. Trustee's Fee	$10.00 or $15.00 for refinancing.
3. Credit Report	$20.00
4. ALTA Inspection*	Flexible costs.
5. Amortization Schedules	$2.00
6. Drafting, notarizing and recording mortgage	$15.00
7. Impounds – Real estate taxes; FHA mortgage insurance; and fire and flood insurance	Flexible costs.
8. Loan Origination Fee	1% on new financing; 2½% on construction of new homes; up to 6 additional points on a refinanced transaction.

*This is a fee charged by the title company to make an inspection only if the property is located in a remote area.

OTHER CLOSING COSTS**

1. Closing Escrow Fee	Flexible Cost.
2. Title Insurance	Flexible Cost.
3. Termite Inspection	Flexible Cost.
4. City Transfer Tax	Flexible Cost.

Discounts allowed include when a builder initiates a mortgage in his own name and is contracting to sell; when a dwelling is constructed by the mortgagor for his own residency; or refinancing a prior mortgage on property owned by the mortgagor.

**Costs paid by the buyer or seller depending on tradition.

BUYER'S COSTS – NOT PERMITTED

1. Prepaid Interest: Interest in excess of the amount due with the first payment.
2. Fees including: tax service, FNMA, warehousing, and loan commitment fees. Also photo and lender's inspection fees.
3. Buyer's and Appliance Warranties.
4. Lender's Appraisal
5. State Revenue Stamps.
6. City Inspection.
7. Disclosure Statement for RESPA.

POINTS

When the market rate for interest is higher than the FHA interest rate, the lender will not make the loan unless he is paid the difference in the form of a loan fee referred to as *points.* The seller's points vary substantially, depending upon the current market rate of interest. Since the buyer is only allowed to pay a maximum loan origination fee of 1%, the seller has to be charged points to complete the transaction.

IMPOUNDS

FHA requirements make it necessary for lenders to collect from the borrower funds to cover real estate taxes and hazard insurance premiums. Lenders will not make loans unless they can determine that these liabilities will be paid when due.

TRUST FUND

Before a loan is funded, the lender will require the buyer to deposit at the close of escrow a certain sum to make the initial tax payment and insurance premiums. The lender will then draw from this trust fund in order to pay necessary tax and insurance premiums when due.

FHA TITLE II-Sec. 203(b) – VETERANS

The FHA program offers veterans low down payments in order to acquire single family dwellings, either existing, proposed or under construction.

ELIGIBILITY

A qualified veteran is one who served at least 90 days of active federal duty in any branch of the armed forces. If a veteran can prove that he served under dangerous conditions, he is eligible with less than the required 90 days.

Veterans are qualified for the FHA program regardless of whether they have obtained a VA Home Loan in the past or if their VA eligibility has expired. Also, this program is available to any veteran an indefinite amount of times.

HOW TO APPLY

A *Certificate of Veterans Status* (Form #26-8261) is requested in addition to standard FHA Sec. 203(b) forms and can be obtained from the Veterans Administration. To obtain this certificate, Veterans must fill out VA Form #26-8261A. It can be acquired at any VA or FHA office and should be mailed along with discharge papers to the VA regional office.

PERCENTAGE OF LOAN TO VALUE

The first $25,000 of appraised value and closing costs is 100% insurable. The remainder is 95% insurable.

Homes not built under HUD/FHA specifications and are less than one year old are 90% insurable on appraised value.

Under this program the veteran must have a minimum of $200 for closing costs and the home being purchased must be a single family residence, owner occuped.

FHA TITLE II-Sec. 207 – RENTAL HOUSING AND MOBILE HOME PARKS

Purpose

To facilitate the production of rental accommodation for families with children at reasonable rents. This is accomplished by offering insurable financing for new construction or rehabilitation of developments having eight or more dwelling units. These projects may be detached, semi-detached or row structures with or without elevators.

This plan is also accessable to mobile home parks. Requirements state that projects must have at least eight home sites in completion or rehabilitation of existing parks. Each site must include the following: side yard, clothes drying facility, paved patio, and sanitary, electrical and water utilities.

Limitations

To provide reasonable rentals to tenants, the Secretary of HUD regulates rents, sales, fees, rate of return and methods of operation involving this program.

In addition, the mortgagor must certify under oath to the Secretary of HUD that he will not discriminate against a family because of children nor will he sell the property while the insurance is in effect. If he does sell, the purchaser must certify to the above restrictions with the Secretary of HUD.

Loans

Note: At the time of this writing the following specifications were relevant; however, because the FHA continues to upgrade its programs, it is important that you check with your local FHA for any changes in this area.

A loan for 90% of estimated value of the property after the development has been completed may be obtained. With the exclusion of exterior land improvements in low cost areas the maximum loan per dwelling unit is as follows:

Type of Unit	*Non-Elevator Projects*	*Elevator Projects*
No Bedroom	$13,000	$15,000
One Bedroom	18,000	21,000
Two Bedrooms	21,500	25,750
Three Bedrooms	26,500	32,250
Four or More Bedrooms	30,000	36,465

Limits may be increased up to 45% for high cost areas.

Maximum loan per mobile home space is $3,250.

FHA TITLE II-Sec. 221(d)(4) – RENTAL HOUSING

Purpose

This plan is instrumental in financing new construction or

the rehabilitation of existing dwellings consisting of five or more units. Units can be detached, semi-detached or row structures, with or without elevators.

The FHA regulates rentals, method of operation and rate of return on projects under this program.

Loans

Note: At the time of this writing the following specifications were relevant; however, because the FHA continues to upgrade its programs, it is important that you check with your local FHA for any changes in this area.

With the exclusion of exterior land improvements in low cost areas, the maximum insurable loan per dwelling is as follows:

Type of Unit	*Non-Elevator Projects*	*Elevator Projects*
No Bedroom	$12,300	$13,975
One Bedroom	17,188	20,025
Two Bedrooms	20,525	24,350
Three Bedrooms	24,700	31,500
Four or More Bedrooms	29,000	34,578

Limits may be increased up to 45% in high cost areas

Percentage of Loan to Value

If a property is to be rehabilitated, a 90% loan will be granted based on approximate cost of restoration plus 90% of the appraised value or 90% of the purchase price, whichever is less.

A total of 100% financing is available for the cost of rehabilitation if the property is owned free and clear. Also, 100% financing is available if the property is to be refinanced plus the existing indebtedness or 90% of the estimated value before restoration.

New construction warrants a loan of 90% of replacement cost of project.

Terms

The maximum term is 40 years or 75% of the outstanding economic life of the property, whichever is less.

The loan origination fee can be no more than one-half of one per cent, application and commitment fee can be no more than three tenths of one per cent combined and the inspection fee can be no more than one half of one per cent.

FHA TITLE II-Sec. 221(d)(2) – REHABILITATION OF LOW COST HOUSING

Purpose

This program provides financing for existing or proposed low cost one to four family housing, or the rehabilitation of such housing. Also financing is available for families shifted by urban renewal or other government actions and single family housing for additional low to moderate income families.

Loans

Note: At the time of this writing the following specifications were relevant; however, because the FHA continues to upgrade its programs, it is important that you check with your local FHA for any changes in this area.

Type of Unit	*Maximum Loan Low Income Area*	*Maximum Loan High Income Area*
Single Family Residence:		
Three Bedrooms	$31,000	$36,000
Four or more Bedrooms	36,000	42,000
Two Family Residence	35,000	45,000
Three Family Residence	48,600	57,600
Four Family Residence	59,400	68,400

To qualify for four or more bedrooms, the family must have at least five persons.

See FHA Sec. 203(b) for additional information.

FHA TITLE II-Sec. 222 – LOANS FOR IN-SERVICE PERSONNEL

Purpose

This program provides insured mortgage financing for the purchase of homes by service members on active duty. During the period of active duty, the mortgage insurance premium is paid by the Armed Forces. Should the service member be discharged or separated from active duty, he must then begin to pay his mortgage insurance premium.

FHA loans under this program may be made only on owner-occupied single family dwellings.

Additional Forms

Aside from the normal application forms required under Sec. 203(b), servicemen must also obtain form #DD–802 (Defense Department form) from their commanding officers.

Loans

The maximum loan is $90,000.

See FHA Sec. 203(b) for additional information.

FHA TITLE II-Sec. 223(f) – EXISTING MULTI-FAMILY BUILDINGS

Purpose

The purpose of this plan is to finance or refinance existing multi-family buildings containing a minimum of 25 units, being at least three years old, with or without elevators.

Loans

Note: At the time of this writing the following specifications were relevant; however, because the FHA continues to upgrade its programs, it is important that you check with your local FHA for any changes in this area.

The maximum loan is 80% of FHA appraised value or 85% of acquisition cost, whichever is less. With the exclusion of exterior land improvements in low cost areas, the maximum loan per dwelling is as follows:

Type of Building	*Non-Elevator*	*Elevator*
No Bedroom	$13,000	$15,000
One Bedroom	18,000	21,000
Two Bedrooms	21,500	25,750
Three Bedrooms	26,500	32,350
Four or more Bedrooms	30,000	36,460

Limits may be increased up to 45% in high cost areas.

When refinancing existing buildings, maximum loans are 80% of FHA appraised value or the total balance of existing loans, whichever is less.

The maximum term of the loan is 35 years or 75% of the remaining economic life of the project, whichever is less.

Loan Commitment Fees

A maximum two tenths of one percent of the requested mortgage for a conditional commitment, and three-tenths of one percent for a firm loan commitment is required.

Rental Income Restrictions

The commissioner of HUD requires that the building must produce sufficient rental income to pay all operating expenses, debt service and a reserve allowance to replace operating equipment.

FHA TITLE II-Sec 234(c) – CONDOMINUMS

Purpose

This plan provides insured mortgage financing for the purchase of individual condominium projects, containing four or more units. A family cannot own more than four units and must occupy at least one.

Loans

The maximum loan is $90,000.

For additional information see FHA Sec. 203(b).

FHA TITLE II-Sec. 234(d) – CONDOMINIUM PROJECTS

This program provides financing for the construction or rehabilitation of multi-family projects including detached, row, walkup or elevator type. They must consist of four or more units and be purchased by a developer who intends to sell individual units as condominiums.

Loans Note: At the time of this writing the following specifications were relevant; however, because the FHA continues to upgrade its programs, it is important that you check with your local FHA for any changes in this area.

Private mortgagors—$20 million maximum.

Public mortgagors—$25 million maximum.

The maximum insurable amounts in low cost areas per unit are as follows:

Type of Unit	*Non-Elevator*	*Elevator*
No Bedroom	$13,000	$15,000
One Bedroom	18,000	21,000
Two Bedrooms	21,500	25,750
Three Bedrooms	26,500	32,250
Four or more Bedrooms	30,000	36,465

Limits may be increased up to 45% in high cost areas.

Percentage of Loan to Value

A loan of 90% of the estimated replacement cost or the sum of maximum insurable units, whichever is less, is attainable for proposed construction. Replacement cost is equivalent to the total cost after all proposed improvements have been made. This consists of items approved by HUD including land and physical betterment, utilities, taxes and architect's fees.

Terms

The maximum term under this program is 40 years or 75%

of the remaining economic life of the property, whichever is less.

Additional Fees

A total of three tenths of one percent is charged for the loan application and committment fee. The inspection fee can be no more than one half of one percent.

See FHA 203(b) for additional information.

FHA TITLE II-Sec. 235 – LOW COST HOUSING ASSISTANCE

Purpose

This plan assists lower income families in acquiring a single family residence, cooperative or condominium units by paying part of an eligible family's mortgage interest payments. The eligible family will pay a minimum of 20% of its monthly adjusted gross income towards principal and interest, taxes, insurance, and FHA mortgage insurance premium. The maximum allowable assistance payment by FHA is the smaller difference between the monthly amount of principal and interest at the current FHA rate and either 20% of the family's adjusted gross income or the monthly amount of principal and interest at 5% per annum.

Eligibility

This program is available to an eligible purchaser who has an adjusted gross income not in excess of 135% of the maximum income limits that can be established in the area for initial occupancy in public housing.

Adjusted gross income is a family's total gross income, including a working wife's income, but not that of any minors, less 5% for payments toward social security, less $300 for each minor under 21 living with the family.

Eligible purchasers are two or more persons related by marriage or blood, occupying the same living unit. Also eligible are handicapped persons and single persons 62 years of age or older.

Down Payment

The down payment required under this program is 3% of FHA appraised value or the acquisition cost, whichever is less.

Loans

Note: At the time of this writing the following specifications were relevant; however, because the FHA continues to upgrade its programs, it is important that you check with your local FHA for any changes in this area.

Single Family Residence	*Low Income Areas*	*High Income Areas*
Three Bedrooms	$32,000	$38,000
Four or more Bedrooms	38,000	44,000

To qualify for four or more bedrooms, the family must have at least five persons.

Terms

Maximum term of this loan is 30 years.

Property Specifications

To qualify for this program residences must be single family dwellings either new or substantially rehabilitated.

A single family unit within a condominum project or rehabilitated two family unit (provided owner lives in one) also qualify.

Reimbursement for Defects

It is required that sellers reimburse HUD for expenses incurred to correct structural defects if they existed and were overlooked when FHA agreed to insure the mortgage.

To make sure HUD is reimbursed, non-occupant sellers must deposit a 5% sales price deposit in escrow.

See FHA Sec. 203(b) for more information.

FHA Sec. 245 – GRADUATED PAYMENT MORTGAGE (GPM)

Purpose

This program offers the home buyer more purchasing power to finance the acquisition of a single family dwelling. This is done by reducing the monthly payments due in the early years of a mortgage, then gradually increase them in later years allowing the home buyer's income to increase.

Requirements and Plans

This form of mortgage plan must meet the same requirements of Sec. 203(b) or Sec. 234-Condominiums with the exceptions listed below.

Plan I – Monthly payments increase at a rate of 2.5% per year for five years

Plan II – Monthly payments increase at a rate of 5% per year for five years

Plan III – Monthly payments increase at a rate of 7.5% per year

Plan IV – Monthly payments increase at a rate of 2% per year for 10 years

Plan V – Monthly payments increase at a rate of 3% per year for 10 years

Due to the new Graduated Payment Mortgage (GPM) plan, often monthly mortgage payments in the early years of the loan are not adequate to cover interest due. Therefore, the unpaid loan balance often increases. In other words, a borrower could conceivably make regular payments on the GPM plan for a number of years and the loan balance could be greater than the original loan amount.

Since current regulations limit the maximum insurable loan amount, it is this greater amount of principal obligation that cannot exceed $90,000 (also the maximum insurable loan amount under equal payment mortgage plans.) To conform to this requirement the minimum down payment under the GPM plan will, in many cases, be greater than that required under equal payment mortgage plans.

Table I on page 80 is used to determine allowable loan amounts and required minimum down payments. It denotes the highest outstanding loan balance with a basis of $1,000 loan and the month when this occurs while utilizing various interest rates and plans.

TABLE I

	Plan I		*Plan II*		*Plan III*		*Plan IV*		*Plan V*	
Rate	*Factor*	*Term*	*Factor*	*Term*	*Factor*	*Term*	*Factor*	*Term*	*Factor*	*Term*
9.50	1004.2870	24	1025.1492	48	1049.5186	48	1014.5779	48	1040.1273	72
9.75	1005.2328	24	1027.5332	48	1052.4179	48	1016.6229	60	1043.7281	72
10.00	1006.1478	24	1029.8654	48	1055.2608	48	1019.0874	60	1047.2378	72
10.25	1007.1437	36	1032.1408	48	1058.0558	48	1021.4769	60	1050.7043	84
10.50	1008.4346	36	1034.3672	48	1060.7925	48	1023.7966	60	1054.6204	84

For a loan on $1,000 at 9.5% interest using Plan I, the highest outstanding loan balance will occur in the twenty-fourth month. At that point the outstanding principal balance will be $1,004.29. (Please note that this figure is only approximate, as a complete amortization schedule is needed to represent an exact amount.)

Amount of Minimum Down Payment

Two calculations are necessary to determine the allowable loan amount, which will also determine the amount of minimum down payment. Of the two calculations, select the lower value, as follows:

1. As per Section 203(b), it is first necessary to find the loan-to-value ratio. This is determined by taking the value of the home plus closing costs, or the acquisition cost and applying it to the loan-to-value ratio. The allowable loan equals 97% of the first $25,000 in value, plus 95% of the excess. For veterans, the allowable loan amount equals 100% of the first $25,000, plus 95% of the excess.

2. The second calculation takes 97% of the estimate of value plus closing cost, or the acquisition cost, which is then divided by the greatest outstanding balance factor (Table I), and multiplied by 1,000. However, if the borrower is a veteran, the total mortgage amount including deferred interest, cannot exceed the restrictions imposed for veterans under Section 230(b).

Examples: Plan III, 9.5%, $60,000

Standard GPM (Non-Veteran)

1. Allowable Loan 203(b) = $25,000 × .97 = $24,250
   $35,000 × .95 = $33,250
   $57,500

2. Allowable Loan $= \frac{\$60,000 \times .97 \times 1,000}{1049.5186} = \$55,454$

Reduce the result to next lower $50 increment which equals $55,450. The mortgage amount will be the lesser of the above two.

The lowest value in the above two calculations is $55,450. This is the maximum insurable loan amount. Now the minimum down payment can be calculated as follows:

Minimum down payment = Acquisition Cost − Loan

or

$4,550 = $60,000 − $55,450

Veteran GPM

1. Allowable Loan = $25,000 × 1.00 = $25,000
   203(b) $35,000 × .95 = $33,250
   $58,250

2. Allowable Loan = $\frac{\$58{,}250 \times 1{,}000}{1049.5186}$ = $55,501.64

Reduce the result to next lower $50 increment which equals $55,500. Mortgage amount will be lesser of the above two.

The lowest value in the above two calculations is $55,500. This is the maximum insurable loan amount. Now the minimum down payment can be calculated as follows:

Minimum down payment = Acquisition Cost − Loan

or

$4,500 = $60,000 − $55,500

IMPORTANT: The calculated minimum down payment for veterans as shown is above the $200 minimum required of veterans. If any of the $200 minimum is not applied to closing costs, add the unused portion to your calculated down payment and also deduct it from the mortgage amount.

FHA TITLE I - MOBILE HOMES

Purpose

To finance the acquisition of new or used mobile homes which must be owner occupied.

Restrictions

The mobile home must be new. If it is used, then the seller must have financied it with an FHA Mobile Home Loan or it is occupied by the buyer under a government lease after having relocated from a previous housing disaster.

Other requirements state the mobile home must have at least 400 square feet, be placed in an approved lot and built to the conditions of the American Standards Institute.

Loans

Loans for a single module is up to $12,500 and $20,000 for a mobile home composed of more than one module.

Terms

Term of the loan is 12 years for a single module and 15 years for a double module mobile home. The FHA charges the buyer .54 of one percent insurance premium on the net loan proceeds to insure the lender against loss.

Allowable Charges

The following charges are allowed when they do not raise the mortgage above the maximum limits prescribed. These are: state and local sales tax, filing and recording fees, stamp taxes, and hazard insurance for up to five years. Transportation and installation charges from the dealer to site are allowed up to $400 for single module and $600 for double module.

Down Payment

The down payment required is 5% on the first $3,000 of purchase price and 10% of any excess. A used mobile home may be used for a down payment when its blue book value equals the minimum down payment required.

Eligibility Requirements

An eligible buyer must have sufficient funds to make a specified down payment and sufficient income to make payments on the loan. The eligible buyer must also specify that he intends to use the mobile home as his principal residence. FHA also requires an acceptable site on which the mobile home is to be placed. Such site may be rented space in a mobile home park, or it may be land owned by the borrower. The site must meet FHA standards, and both buyer and seller must certify that there will be no violation of zoning requirements or other regulations applicable to mobile homes.

An eligible mobile home must be at least 10 feet wide and 30 feet long, or shall consist of a module or modules having a minimum floor space area of at least 400 square feet. It must meet FHA construction standards for mobile homes. It also must be new; if not new, it must have been formerly financed with an FHA insured loan. The total price of a mobile home may include furnishings, appliances, tie-downs and also include setting up of mobile home at site where it will be occupied, and initial premium for insurance on mobile home.

VA FINANCING

PURPOSE

This program under the direction of the Veterans Administration guarantees loans made by private lenders to eligible veterans. If no private financing is available, the VA will make direct loans to veterans.

The VA will guarantee loans on the following types of property: one to four family dwellings, single family dwellings including condominiums, and mobile homes and mobile home lots.

VETERANS ELIGIBLE

Eligible veterans are those with a minimum of 90 days active duty in the armed forces during World War II (September 16,

1940, to July 25, 1947) or during the Korean Conflict (June 27, to January 31, 1955).

Veterans whose active duty transpired between July 25, 1947, and June 27, 1950, or any time after January 31, 1955, are required a minimum of 180 days active duty.

Only those veterans discharged under other than dishonorable conditions or because of service-connected disability are eligible.

Unmarried spouses of veterans who served during above periods and have service related deaths are also eligible.

Additionally, certain citizens of the United States who served in the armed forces of an allied foreign government during World War II are eligible.

HOW TO APPLY

A veteran may apply for a Certificate of Eligibility at any regional VA office. This request should be accompanied by his discharge papers (Form DD-214) or evidence of current active duty status.

APPRAISED VALUE

Once the eligible veteran finds the property that will accommodate VA financing, the VA will appraise the property and issue a Certificate of Reasonable Value (CRV). The amount of the loan guaranteed cannot exceed the CRV, including construction, alteration or repairs.

LOAN GUARANTY

Currently there is no limitation on the amount of a loan

eligible for a VA loan guaranty. However, there is a restriction on the amount of guaranty that can be issued.

The maximum guaranty for a loan to finance the purchase of a dwelling is 60% of the loan amount or $27,500, whichever is less. This also applies to construction or alteration of a dwelling.

Additionally, a loan guaranty of up to 60% of the loan amount but not exceeding $27,500 is authorized to refinance existing liens of record in owner-occupied homes by eligible veterans.

TERMS

Discount points charged by lenders on refinance loans must be approved by the VA and cannot exceed points currently being charged for other VA loans.

The VA does not have any loan limtis, only limits on the amount of guaranty. The Government National Mortgage Association and FNMA purchase seasoned VA mortgages from lenders, provided that the loan amount is in proportion to the veteran's entitlement to loan guaranty. These loan to guaranty ratios established by GNMA and FNMA are currently four times the maximum of $27,500, or $110,000.

LOANS

When a veteran is still liable for his previous VA loan, wherein he may still own his own home or has allowed a new buyer to assume the existing mortgage, the following is the method for computing the maximum VA loan the lender will make on a new home based on his remaining entitlement.

The maximum loan is equivalent entitlement plus 75% of the CRV or the purchase price, whichever is less. For example: assume a veteran bought a home in 1968 and used his VA entitlement. (The maximum VA loan guaranty in 1968 was $12,500). Then in 1979, that same veteran decided to rent his home and purchase a new home for $80,000 with a CRV equal to the purchase price. What is the maximum VA loan attainable and how much of a down payment does he need to finance his new home?

Answer: Maximum loan guaranty in 1979	$25,000
Less maximum loan guaranty in 1968	$12,500
Remaining veteran entitlement	$12,500
Plus 75% of the $80,000 CRV	$60,000
Equals maximum loan obtainable	$72,500

Therefore, at a purchase price of $80,000 the veteran would need a cash down payment of $7,500.

ENTITLEMENT

The Veterans Administration permits entire restoration of a veteran's full entitlement of the current maximum guarantee of $27,500 if the property has been sold and the previous loan has been paid in full. The veteran will also receive full entitlement should the property be sold to another veteran who assumes the existing VA loan with release of liability and agrees to use his own entitlement.

Even though a veteran may already have an existing VA loan, he can still purchase a new home without selling his old home as long as his entitlement varies substantially from his original entitlement. For example, if he bought his original home with a maximum loan gurantee of $7,500, the remaining entitlement would be $20,000, which is the difference between the current maximum guaranty of $27,500 and the maximum of $7,500 at the time his original home was financed.

OCCUPANCY REQUIREMENT

Certification of Intention of the veteran to occupy the home he is about to purchase is required by the VA before the loan will be made. However, should the veteran later move to another home, he may rent his old home financed by the VA loan.

BUYER QUALIFICATION

The VA does not use specific ratios to qualify the veteran buyer. However, the following guide can normally be used to estimate whether or not the buyer will qualify for a VA loan: the monthly income of both husband and wife less monthly debt payments should equal four times the monthly payment of the purchased home. Monthly payments include principal, interest, insurance, real estate taxes and special assessments.

The veteran's job stability and credit worthiness are considered along with present and anticipated income. Overtime pay is not taken into account regarding long-term projections to meet loan payments, but is considered against short-term debt obligations.

Additionally, the VA does not accept co-signers and co-mortgagors.

DOWN PAYMENT

The VA does not require a down payment by the veteran. However, should the veteran agree to purchase a home in excess of the Certificate of Reasonable Value issued by the VA, he is requested to pay such excess in cash.

CLOSING COSTS

Closing costs must be paid in cash at the close of escrow and cannot be included in the loan.

VA Regulation 36:4312 prohibits excessive closing costs be charged to the veteran buyer for the purchase, construction, repair, alteration or improvement of residential property. This regulation prepares a schedule for allowable closing costs.

POINTS

When the market rate for interest is higher than the VA interest rate, the lender will not make the loan unless he is paid the difference in the form of a loan fee referred to as points. Since the buyer is only allowed to pay a maximum loan orignation fee of one percent, the seller has to be charged points to complete the transaction.

IMPOUNDS

VA requirements make it necessary for lenders to collect from the borrower funds to cover real estate taxes and hazard insurance premiums. Lenders will not make loans unless they can determine that these liabilities will be paid when due.

TRUST FUND

Before a loan is funded, the lender will require the buyer to deposit at the close of escrow a certain sum to make the initial tax payment and insurance premiums. The lender will then draw from his trust fund in order to pay necessary tax and insurance premiums when they are due.

PREPAYMENT PENALTY

If a VA loan is partially or fully repaid at any time prior to the end of the term, there is no prepayment penalty.

VA—MOBILE HOMES

VA is authorized to guarantee loans made by private lenders to eligible veterans for the purchase of new or used mobile homes with or without a lot. The guaranty on a mobile home loan will be an amount equal to the veteran's available entitlement, not to exceed the maximum $20,000 or 50%, whichever is less. A veteran who already owns a mobile home may obtain a VA guaranteed loan to purchase a lot on which to place the mobile home.

Veterans who receive a guaranteed mobile home loan can use their full entitlement to buy a standard home, if their mobile home loan is paid off in full.

VA interest rates for mobile home loans vary from those established for conventional home loans.

Loan terms for the purchase of a new single-wide mobile home, with or without a lot, or a loan to purchase a lot only, is limited to a maximum of 15 years and 32 days. A loan for the purchase of a new double-wide mobile home, with or without a lot, has a maximum term of 20 years and 32 days. The maximum term for used units may not exceed the preceeding units or the remaining physical life of the unit as determined by the VA, whichever is less.

It is likely that the VA will establish maximum loans

within the above limits to require the veteran to place a 10% down payment when purchasing a mobile home.

An approved mobile home must be minimum size of 40′ X 10′, constructed for towing, equipped for year-round living, and conform to the specifications of the American National Standard Institute (ANSI) standard #A-119.1.

ASSUMING & TAKING SUBJECT TO A MORTGAGE

ASSUMING A MORTGAGE

When a new buyer assumes a mortgage, a formal agreement between buyer and lender is executed. Often, the new buyer will be faced with an increased interest rate, along with an assumption fee, subject to approval of his credit.

The actual assumption transfers the responsibility of the mortgage payment from the seller to the new owner. Savings and loan associations and commercial banks will usually insist on formal assumption of the existing mortgage because they most often include due-on-sale clauses in their mortgage instruments.

TAKING SUBJECT TO A MORTGAGE

A property is taken subject to a mortgage when there is no

agreement between the lender and the new purchaser of the property. This can technically only occur when the note contains no due-on-sale clause, as in the case of VA, FHA, and most insurance loans. Therefore, when there is no due-on-sale clause, the lender's consent to the transfer is not necessary.

When the buyer takes subject to a mortgage, the primary responsibility for payment of the mortgage is the original maker of the note. Since the lender only has a contractual agreement with the original borrower, the new owner is not technically obligated to pay off the mortgage debt because he never agreed to in writing. The only time there is a reason for concern by the seller is when the new buyer has a thin equity position in the property. In the event of default, the lender would foreclose and then sell the property. If there are enough proceeds from the sale to satisfy the balance owing on the mortgage the original borrower will be released from all obligations on the mortgage. If the property does not yield sufficient proceeds to cover the loan balance, the lender may have legal recourse to recover the deficiency, depending on individual state laws of where the property is located.

Savings and loan associations and commercial banks will usually insist on formal assumption of the existing mortgage because they most often include due-on-sale clauses in their mortgage instruments. The new buyer may be faced with an increased interest rate, depending on the prevailing market rate, along with an assumption fee, subject to approval of credit.

Life insurance companies usually do not include due-on-sale clauses in their mortgage instruments, mainly because of their long term investment objectives. However, they do charge large prepayment penalties and will often lock-in the mortgage, which disallows early payoff of the mortgage under any circumstances.

ALL-INCLUSIVE TRUST DEED

The All-Inclusive Trust Deed (AITD) is a security instrument similar to a Land Contract, except that the title to the property is actually transfered and the existing encumbrances to which it is subordinated. The buyer will become the trustor on the all inclusive note and trust deed while the seller becomes the beneficiary. It also is commonly referred to as an *overlapping deed of trust.*

In essence, the existing loans remain intact while the buyer begins making payment to the seller, then in turn the seller continues to make payments on the existing encumbrances to the original lender.

This can only be used when there is no form of alienation clause prevailing in any of the notes or trust deeds which remain on the subject property.

The AITD is most desirable when the seller wishes to benefit from his present low interest loans; but is still anxious to sell. The seller can write the AITD with a higher interest rate over and above the existing interest rates on the present loans thereby benefiting from the spread in rates.

It is also advantageous when the seller is anxious to sell but is faced with a buyer who has a small down payment or when the money market is *tight* and it is unlikely the buyer will qualify for a new loan.

EXAMPLE OF EFFECTIVE INTEREST YIELD ON AN AITD

Assume a seller wishes to sell a property for $100,000 using an All-Inclusive Trust Deed and he has existing financing on the property which consists of the following: A first trust deed of $40,000 at 7% and a second trust deed of $20,000 at 8%. His existing encumbrances total $60,000; therefore his seller's equity equals $40,000. So if he offers to sell this property with an AITD at 10% with a $10,000 down payment, then his effective yield would be calculated as follows:

Seller gets 10% × $90,000 = $9,000 interest
and pays 7% × $40,000
8% × $20,000 = $4,400 interest

Therefore, the seller nets $4,600 interest on equity of $40,000 or an effective interest yield of 11.5%.

ADVANTAGES TO THE SELLER

1. The seller will get a much higher effective interest on value of the AITD (see example of effective interest yield) without being classified as being usurious.
2. It is an effective method of selling property which has a locked-in loan against it, without negotiating with

the existing lender for loan assumption or additional financing.

3. Since the AITD generates a higher effective interest rate than a similar purchase money trust deed it can be cashed for a lower discount rate.
4. The seller can get a higher price for the property by offering better terms available through an AITD.
5. In the case of repossession, an AITD is better than a Land Contract, because the property can be regained through a Trustee Sale, while a Land Contract often requires a court judgement.

ADVANTAGES TO THE BUYER

1. The buyer can acquire a property with a small down payment, without new loan origination fees, often at an interest rate below the prevailing rate.
2. Title to the property is received as opposed to a Land Contract.
3. AITD saves time required to shop and apply for a new loan and is only responsible for one loan payment.

PRECAUTIONARY MEASURES FOR PROTECTION OF THE SELLER

1. Forbid the use of another AITD in the event of resale of the subject property.
2. The seller should retain the right to approve all leases which might have a detrimental effect on the value of the property.
3. An impound account should be made available to pay taxes and insurance.
4. Provide loan due dates to accommodate payment of funds required for existing senior loan due dates.

5. Circumstances that will cause default, the amount which will be in default, and the exact procedure to be followed upon foreclosure should be defined.

FOR THE PROTECTION OF THE BUYER

1. To avoid the possibility of the property being lost due to failure of the seller to make payments on the existing senior loans, a neutral trust or collection agency should be made responsible for receiving payments from the buyer, then making existing loan payments for the seller. Cost of such an arrangement as well as who should pay for it have to be considered.
2. The buyer could have the right to assume one or all of the existing senior loans of record upon the occurrence of a certain event, such as a balloon payment.

POINTS TO REMEMBER

When an AITD is used, the buyer takes the property subject to the existing liens while the seller remains the trustor. This can only be accomplished when such liens are not due-on-sale. Furthermore, the AITD is recorded as a junior lien subject to the existing liens.

FINANCING WITH NO MONEY DOWN

When you initiate a new loan on real estate through a conventional lender, it will usually require a substantial down payment. Lenders frown on buyers borrowing the down payment because it can erode their security in the property. But when you assume existing VA or FHA financing there is no credit qualification and the existing lender does not verify where the down payment comes from. This is usually the case when a Land Contract is arranged and the seller is lenient with credit requirements.

Therefore, assuming a three bedroom home is located that can be purchased for $60,000 and there exists a VA loan on the home for $50,000, which the seller will allow to be assumed, there are one of two options to purchase this home with no money down. The seller could carry a second mortgage for $10,000, or the buyer can borrow this amount for a short term from various sources.

If the seller carries a second mortgage, which is by far the least complicated, then all the financing problems with no down payment are solved. But if the seller wants his $10,000 cash out of the property immediately at the close of escrow, another interested party (like the real estate agent) can buy the second mortgage from the seller at a discounted rate, and both the buyer and seller have solved the problem of financing. For the seller to still get his $10,000 cash out of the property it will be necessary for the buyer to increase the amount paid for the home by an amount equal to that of the discount of the second mortgage. In other words, if the buyer of the second mortgage will discount the note by 20% then the face value of the note will have to be sufficient enough that when it is discounted, it will yield $10,000 in cash to the seller of the property.

In this particular case, the face value of the note would have to be $12,500 after being discounted 20%. Therefore, you would end up paying $62,500 for the house, instead of $60,000, so that the seller would have his cash out of the transaction.

When borrowing the down payment outright, without involvement of the seller, the funds can initially be appropriated from one or a number of sources for the short term. Then, once the buyer gains possession of the property, a long term second mortgage can be taken out and all the loans incurred to acquire the property can be paid off.

The purpose of taking out a longer term loan after acquisition is to lower monthly payments and get the benefits of a lower interest rate loan which is available when it's secured by real property. Then, once the property is rented, the income should adequately compensate the buyer over and above all mortgage payments and expenses.

SECONDARY FINANCING

An owner of real estate is entitled to arrange more than one loan against the same property through financial instruments of *Second Mortgages* and *Second Trust Deeds.* These "junior" or "subordinate" loans are called "second" because they are second in priority to first loans with respect to claims upon the proceeds from the act of foreclosure. Additional loans, "thirds" etc., would be lower in priority as compared to second and first loans.

SOURCES FOR SECONDARY FINANCING

The most common situation is when the seller of real property is willing to accept a note from the buyer, which is secured by a second deed of trust or mortgage on the property sold.

Private investors often purchase notes secured by deeds of trust or mortgages on real property. Normally, these notes are purchased for cash, at a discount from the face value in order to raise the yield of the note.

Additionally, real estate brokers often act as loan brokers in placing second loans for a fee or commission.

MARKET FOR SECONDS

Notes secured by mortgages or second deeds of trust on real property are negotiable instruments which have a cash value that is typically lower than the face value of the note. This variance between face value and cash value is referred to as the *discount*.

Investors of these negotiable notes expect a certain constant yield from their invested capital. Therefore, the discounts associated with these notes varies in proportion with the terms of the note, the trustor's equity in the property, his credit history, as well as quality and condition of the property.

TERMS OF NOTES

The following items are essential to create the terms of a note:

1. Annual interest rate.
2. The amount of monthly payments including principal and interest, presented in percentages of the face value of the note. Most commonly one percent of the face value is paid monthly by the borrower.
3. Due date—the date the entire remaining balance becomes due and payable in full.
4. Transferability—whether or not the note has an expressed acceleration clause stating that the note becomes immediately due and payable in full should the borrower sell or transfer the property.

FINANCIAL DISCLOSURE—TRUTH IN LENDING ACT

The purpose of the *Truth in Lending Act,* Regulation Z/226.1 (a)(1), is to let borrowers and customers know the cost of credit so that they can compare costs with those of other sources and avoid the uninformed use of credit. Regulation Z does not fix maximum, minimum or any charges for credit.

The finance charge and the annual percentage rate are really the two most important disclosures required by this regulation. These two items tell the customer, at a glance, how much he is paying for his credit and its relative cost in percentage terms.

At one time, a lender may have stated that he would offer a consumer loan of $1,000 at 6% interest for a term of one year. He would then charge the borrower $60 for the loan, deduct it from the $1,000, and give the remaining balance of $940 to the borrower. Since the actual effective interest rate on $940 paying back $1,000, is in effect 6.38%, not 6%, is actually one of the major reasons why truth in lending came into existence.

WHO IT APPLIES TO

Regulation Z applies to banks, savings and loan associations, department stores, credit card issuers, credit unions, automobile dealers, consumer finance companies, residential mortgage brokers, and craftsmen such as plumbers and electricians. It also applies to doctors, dentists, and other professional people, and hospitals. In fact, it applies to any individual or organization that extends or arranges credit for which a finance charge is, or may be payable, or which is repayable in more than four installments.

TYPES OF CREDIT COVERED

Generally speaking, credit that is extended to people for personal, family, household or agricultural purposes, not exceeding $2,000 is covered under Regulation Z. However, all real estate credit transactions for these purposes are covered regardless of the amount.

TYPES OF CREDIT NOT COVERED

The following are not affected by Regulation Z.

1. Business and commercial credit, except agricultural credit.
2. Credit to federal, state and local governments. However, governmental units extending credit to individuals are affected by this law.
3. Transactions in securities and commodities accounts with a broker-dealer registered with the Securities & Exchange Commission.
4. Transactions under certain public utility tariffs.
5. Credit over $25,000, except real estate transactions.

Credit terms which are advertised to the consumer must comply with certain requirements and these terms cannot be advertised unless the creditor customarily extends such terms. Terms advertised means any commercial message applied to the following media including any direct mail, newspaper, magazine, leaflet or catalog, radio broadcast, television or system of public address. Also included are any printed material on any interior or exterior window sign, any handout literature, or price tag which is made available to customers or prospective customers in any manner whatsoever.

ENFORCEMENT

Specific responsibilities for enforcement of Regulation Z are divided among nine federal agencies. A complete list of these agencies and the types of businesses they cover are as follows:

National Banks – Controller of the Currency, United States Treasury Department, Washington, D.C. 20220

State Member Banks – Federal Reserve Bank serving the area in which the state member bank is located.

Non-member Insured Banks – Federal Deposit Insurance Corporation Supervising Examiner for the District in which the non-member insured bank is located.

Savings Institutions – Insured by the FSLIC and members of the FHLB system (except for savings banks insured by FDIC). The FHLB's supervisory agent in the Federal Home Loan Bank District in which the institution is located.

Federal Credit Unions – Regional Office of the Bureau for Federal Credit Unions, serving the area in which the Federal Credit Union is located.

Creditors Subject to Civil Aeronautics Board – Director, Bureau of Enforcement, Civil Aeronautics Board, 1825 Connecticut Avenue, N.W. Washington, D.C. 20428

Creditors Subject to Interstate Commerce Commission – Office of Proceedings, Interstate Commerce Commission, Washington, D.C. 20523

Creditors Subject to Packers and Stockyard Act – Nearest Packers and Stockyards Administration area supervisor.

Retail, Department Stores, Consumer Finance Companies and all other creditors – Truth in Lending, Federal Trade Commission, Washington, D.C. 20580.

PENALTIES

If a creditor fails to make disclosures as required under this regulation, the affected consumer may sue for twice the amount of the finance charge for a minimum of $100, up to a maximum of $1,000 plus court costs and attorney fees. Also, if a creditor willfully or knowingly disobeys the law or Regulation Z and is convicted, he could be fined up to $5,000, or be imprisoned for one year, or both.

ANNUAL PERCENTAGE RATE (APR) DEFINED

It is the relative cost of credit in percentage terms. It must be stated accurately to the nearest one quarter of one percent on the unpaid balance of the amount financed.

FINANCE CHARGE DEFINED

It is the total of all costs which the consumer must pay, directly or indirectly for obtaining credit. The following are some of the more common items that must be included in the finance charge:

1. Interest.
2. Loan fee.
3. Finder's fee or similar charge.
4. Time price differential.
5. Amount paid as a discount.
6. Service, transaction or carrying charge.
7. Points.
8. Appraisal fee (except in real estate transactions).
9. Premium for credit life or other insurance, should this be a condition for giving credit.
10. Investigation or credit report fee (except in real estate transactions).

The following are certain costs which are often paid even when credit is not employed and may be excluded, but may be itemized and shown to the consumer:

1. Taxes.
2. License fees.
3. Registration fees.
4. Certain title and other legal fees.
5. Some real estate closing fees.

APR AND FINANCE CHARGE MUST BE CLEAR

The finance charge must be clearly typed or written, stating the dollars and cents total and the annual percentage rate. The words "finance charge" and "annual percentage rate" must stand out especially clear. In the sale of dwellings, the total dollar finance charge need not be stated, although the annual percentage rate must be included.

REGULATION Z AND REAL ESTATE LOANS

All real estate credit in any amount is covered under this

regulation when it is to an individual and not for business purposes, unless the business purpose is agriculture. Any credit transaction that involves any type of security interest in real estate of a consumer is covered.

A special provision with regards to real estate allows the lender not to have to show the total amount of the finance charge on a credit sale, or first mortgage loan to finance the purchase of the consumer's dwelling. Also, the consumer has the right to cancel a credit arrangement within three business days if his residence is used as security for the credit.

A consumer may cancel a transaction by signing and dating the notice which he can receive from the creditor, and either mail the notice to the creditor, personally deliver it, send it by messenger or by telegram. A brief description of the transaction which the consumer wishes to cancel should be included in the telegram.

Another method of cancelling is to prepare a letter that includes a brief description of the transaction and deliver it to the credit in the same fashion as the correspondence mentioned above.

A first mortgage to finance the purchase of a residence carries no right to cancel credit arrangements. However, a first mortgage for any other purpose and a second mortgage on the same residence may be cancelled.

YIELD

The meaning of the true yield in relation to all types of real estate loans is often not properly understood by lenders, borrowers, and real estate investors.

Let's make one point very clear. Determining the yield on many loans is far more complex than a mere division problem. The actual calculation itself can be so complex that it requires a computer, a small sophisticated calculator, or computer prepared factors. The formula is too involved to explain, but here is an example.

A person borrows $1,000 for one year and at the end of that year $100 interest is paid. That is 10% interest and it's also a yield of 10%. A key point here is a true yield is always expressed as an annual figure.

Why is the yield and the interest rate the same? Because there were no payments whatsoever made and the term of the loan was a full year, and at the end of that year a certain amount is paid for the use of that money. Divide the cost of the money by the money borrowed:

$$1000\,\overline{)\,100.00\,}\quad .10 \text{ or } 10\% \text{ interest rate or yield}$$

This is the only time the yield is determined by a simple division when no payments are made and the term is a full year (or more than one full year—two years, etc.) and there are no extra charges like escrow fees, loan fees, etc.

Now we can explore some problems that begin to get complex.

$1000 is borrowed for one year and $8.33 is paid each month for 11 months with a final payment of $8.33 plus the $1000 borrowed. However, an extra loan fee of $50 is required to receive the loan. As a result the borrower only receives $950 at the beginning. This is a very different problem.

Let's review it. . . .

The interest paid is still $100 for one year's use of the money. The interest of $100 should not be divided by $950 to get a yield of 10.53 because it can only be used on terms of one year. The interest rate is 10% (100 ÷ 1000), however, the yield must show the relationship between the interest paid ($100), the amount borrowed ($1000) and the extra fees paid ($50) and when the interest and fees are paid. This requires the complex formula discussed.

Since you must spread the $50 fee over a short one year period, the yield in this case is 15.43%. If the same payment is made for two years instead of one and the loan fee and amount of loan remain the same the yield is then 12.85. The effect of the loan fee is spread out over a two-year versus a one-year term. For a three-year term, the yield would be less than 12% . . . 11.99% to be exact.

One is not expected to understand the mathematics involved (few do), only the concept that extra fees (over and above interest) increase the cost of the loan and increase the yield or true annual percentage rate.

The whole area of borrowing a specific amount of money and receiving less than borrowed will always affect the yield. On the above problem, $1000 was borrowed and only $950 was received. This leads into a whole area of yields on discounted notes, trust deeds, and mortgages.

In this area it is not uncommon for individuals to

lend money, then turn around and sell that loan to another party at a discount. Perhaps an example will illustrate this.

You lend person A $10,000 at 11% interest for 23 monthly payments of $125.00 per month and a final payment of $91.10 plus interest for the last monthly period.

Now you decide you need money and want to sell the loan to person B. B says, I want to make more money than 11%. B wants to yield a minimum of 15%. In order for B to do so, A will have to discount the amount of the loan to B. But how much?

To show how much, we will refer to page 231 of "Mortgage Yield Tables" for the precise answers. This page covers 11% - 24 month loans. Look at the third column headed by 1.25, which means the monthly payment is 1.25% of the amount borrowed.

See excerpt of page 231 of "Mortgage Yield Tables" on page 113.

$$10{,}000 \overline{)125.00} = .0125 \text{ or } 1.25\%$$

Follow this column down until you reach a figure in excess of 15.00%. That figure is $15.25. Proceed to the left along that row until you reach the Discount % column. That figure is 7.0%. That means you have to discount the loan 7% or $70 to yield 15.25% [.07 × 10,000 = 70.00].

As you can see from the remainder of the page, the greater the discount given, the higher the yield. Why is this?

The answer is really simple. You are receiving the same monthly payment on a small loan amount. If the loan amount increased and the monthly payment remains the same, your yield will decrease (or less than 11%).

If the yield increases, you are either receiving a larger loan payment on the same loan or you are receiving the same payment on a smaller loan. In either case, the person buying the loan is receiving more benefits, hence the higher yield.

On investments, the higher the yield the better the benefits to the lender, and the greater the dollar return.

On loans, the greater the yield or annual percentage rate, the greater the cost of the loan. The larger the extra fees (over the interest) the greater the cost. The more you spread those costs paid at the beginning over longer terms, the less the yield. Our first example clearly illustrated this concept.

DISCOUNT %	MONTHLY PAYBACK RATE (%) (MONTHLY PAYMENT DIVIDED BY LOAN AMOUNT)										
	.92	1.00	1.25	1.50	1.75	2.00	2.50	3.00	3.50	4.00	4.66
.5	11.28	11.28	11.29	11.30	11.31	11.32	11.35	11.37	11.40	11.44	11.50
1.0	11.56	11.57	11.59	11.60	11.62	11.65	11.69	11.75	11.81	11.89	12.01
1.5	11.85	11.85	11.88	11.91	11.94	11.97	12.04	12.12	12.22	12.33	12.52
2.0	12.13	12.14	12.18	12.22	12.26	12.30	12.39	12.50	12.63	12.79	13.03
2.5	12.42	12.43	12.48	12.52	12.57	12.63	12.75	12.89	13.05	13.24	13.55
3.0	12.71	12.72	12.78	12.83	12.90	12.96	13.10	13.27	13.47	13.70	14.08
3.5	13.00	13.02	13.08	13.15	13.22	13.29	13.46	13.66	13.89	14.16	14.60
4.0	13.29	13.31	13.38	13.46	13.54	13.63	13.82	14.05	14.31	14.62	15.13
4.5	13.58	13.61	13.69	13.78	13.87	13.97	14.19	14.44	14.74	15.09	15.66
5.0	13.88	13.91	14.00	14.09	14.20	14.31	14.55	14.84	15.17	15.56	16.20
5.5	14.17	14.21	14.31	14.41	14.53	14.65	14.92	15.23	15.60	16.04	16.74
6.0	14.47	14.51	14.62	14.74	14.86	15.00	15.29	15.64	16.04	16.51	17.29
6.5	14.77	14.81	14.93	15.06	15.20	15.34	15.67	16.04	16.48	16.99	17.84
7.0	15.08	15.12	15.25	15.39	15.53	15.69	16.04	16.45	16.92	17.48	18.39
7.5	15.38	15.42	15.56	15.71	15.87	16.04	16.42	16.86	17.37	17.97	18.95
8.0	15.69	15.73	15.88	16.04	16.21	16.40	16.80	17.27	17.81	18.46	19.52
8.5	15.99	16.05	16.21	16.38	16.56	16.75	17.18	17.68	18.27	18.96	20.08
9.0	16.30	16.36	16.53	16.71	16.90	17.11	17.57	18.10	18.72	19.46	20.66
9.5	16.61	16.67	16.85	17.05	17.25	17.47	17.96	18.52	19.18	19.96	21.23
10.0	16.93	16.99	17.18	17.39	17.60	17.84	18.35	18.95	19.64	20.47	21.81
10.5	17.24	17.31	17.51	17.73	17.96	18.20	18.75	19.37	20.11	20.98	22.40
11.0	17.56	17.63	17.84	18.07	18.31	18.57	19.14	19.81	20.58	21.50	22.99
11.5	17.88	17.95	18.18	18.41	18.67	18.94	19.54	20.24	21.05	22.02	23.58
12.0	18.20	18.28	18.51	18.76	19.03	19.31	19.95	20.68	21.53	22.54	24.18
12.5	18.53	18.61	18.85	19.11	19.39	19.69	20.35	21.12	22.01	23.07	24.79
13.0	18.85	18.93	19.19	19.47	19.76	20.07	20.76	21.56	22.50	23.60	25.40
13.5	19.18	19.27	19.53	19.82	20.12	20.45	21.17	22.01	22.99	24.14	26.01
14.0	19.51	19.60	19.88	20.18	20.49	20.83	21.59	22.46	23.48	24.68	26.63
14.5	19.84	19.94	20.23	20.54	20.87	21.22	22.01	22.91	23.97	25.23	27.26
15.0	20.18	20.27	20.58	20.90	21.24	21.61	22.43	23.37	24.47	25.78	27.89
15.5	20.51	20.61	20.93	21.26	21.62	22.00	22.85	23.83	24.98	26.33	28.52
16.0	20.85	20.96	21.28	21.63	22.00	22.40	23.28	24.30	25.49	26.89	29.17
16.5	21.19	21.30	21.64	22.00	22.39	22.80	23.71	24.77	26.00	27.45	29.81
17.0	21.54	21.65	22.00	22.37	22.77	23.20	24.14	25.24	26.52	28.02	30.47
17.5	21.88	22.00	22.36	22.75	23.16	23.60	24.58	25.72	27.04	28.60	31.12
18.0	22.23	22.35	22.73	23.13	23.55	24.01	25.02	26.20	27.56	29.18	31.79
18.5	22.58	22.70	23.09	23.51	23.95	24.42	25.47	26.68	28.09	29.76	32.46
19.0	22.93	23.06	23.46	23.89	24.35	24.83	25.92	27.17	28.63	30.35	33.14
19.5	23.29	23.42	23.83	24.28	24.75	25.25	26.37	27.66	29.17	30.95	33.82
20.0	23.65	23.78	24.21	24.66	25.15	25.67	26.82	28.16	29.71	31.55	34.51
21.0	24.37	24.52	24.97	25.45	25.97	26.52	27.74	29.16	30.82	32.76	35.90
22.0	25.10	25.26	25.74	26.25	26.80	27.38	28.68	30.18	31.94	34.00	37.33
23.0	25.85	26.01	26.52	27.06	27.64	28.26	29.63	31.22	33.08	35.26	38.78
24.0	26.60	26.78	27.31	27.88	28.50	29.15	30.60	32.28	34.24	36.55	40.25
25.0	27.37	27.55	28.12	28.72	29.37	30.06	31.59	33.36	35.43	37.86	41.76
26.0	28.15	28.34	28.94	29.57	30.25	30.98	32.59	34.46	36.64	39.19	43.30
27.0	28.94	29.14	29.77	30.43	31.15	31.91	33.61	35.58	37.87	40.56	44.87
28.0	29.74	29.95	30.61	31.31	32.06	32.87	34.65	36.72	39.12	41.95	46.47
29.0	30.56	30.78	31.47	32.21	32.99	33.84	35.71	37.88	40.41	43.37	48.10
30.0	31.39	31.62	32.34	33.11	33.94	34.82	36.79	39.06	41.71	44.82	49.77
31.0	32.23	32.47	33.23	34.04	34.90	35.83	37.89	40.27	43.05	46.29	51.48
32.0	33.08	33.34	34.13	34.98	35.88	36.85	39.01	41.50	44.41	47.81	53.22
33.0	33.95	34.22	35.05	35.93	36.88	37.89	40.15	42.76	45.80	49.35	55.00
34.0	34.84	35.12	35.98	36.91	37.90	38.96	41.31	44.04	47.22	50.93	56.82
35.0	35.74	36.03	36.94	37.90	38.93	40.04	42.50	45.35	48.67	52.54	58.69
36.0	36.66	36.96	37.90	38.91	39.99	41.15	43.72	46.69	50.16	54.20	60.60
37.0	37.59	37.91	38.89	39.94	41.07	42.27	44.96	48.06	51.68	55.89	62.56
38.0	38.54	38.87	39.90	40.99	42.17	43.42	46.22	49.46	53.23	57.62	64.56
39.0	39.51	39.85	40.92	42.06	43.29	44.60	47.52	50.90	54.82	59.40	66.61
40.0	40.50	40.85	41.97	43.16	44.43	45.80	48.84	52.36	56.45	61.22	68.72
	PERCENTAGE OF LOAN AMOUNT LEFT UNPAID AT DUE DATE										
	100.0	97.77	91.10	84.42	77.74	71.07	57.71	44.36	31.00	17.65	.00

LEVERAGE AND BORROWED MONEY

The principle of leverage states that a lower down payment invested in a property and the more financed, the return on the investment will be much greater than with a larger down payment. Leverage is essentially using a small amount of capital to control a larger amount of assets or using borrowed money to make money.

Assume that a person desires to purchase a home for \$100,000 and is fortunate enough to have enough cash to buy it without any financing. The question is . . . should he pay cash for this home or place \$20,000 down and finance the remaining \$80,000?

From an investment standpoint, a 20% down payment would yield a higher return than a 100% cash purchase price for the following reasons. Assume there is a minimum 10% appreciation on the new home annually. Therefore, with a 20% down payment, a 50% return on the investment would be expected (\$100,000 × 10% divided by \$20,000 = 50%). If the home is paid for in cash the return on investment would only yield 10% ($100,000 × 10% divided by $100,000 = 10%).

With any rate of appreciation whatsoever in real estate, using leverage will always out-yield a cash purchase price with respect to return on investment. In fact, the lower the down payment, the higher the return on investment received.

Of course, there are other considerations to be made. Those consumers on fixed wage incomes must consider monthly payments on their home investment. The more leverage that is utilized, the larger the monthly payment will be; and vice versa, the larger the down payment, the smaller the monthly payment required. Another fact to consider is that the interest paid on the loan is tax deductible.

Remember that anyone can emulate the great real estate tycoons by using leverage. Once a substantial amount of equity is derived from initial investments, additional properties can be purchased by taking out loans against that equity.

Land continues to be man's favorite investment. And as population growth continues to seek the finite supply of that land, its value will endure to return to its possessor a bounty of riches. Hopefully, those of you who apply the knowledge gained in this text will expand your horizons and become members of an elite class of people who can return, at day's end, to that wonderful parcel of earth which belongs solely to you, and has been known for centuries as "home sweet home."

****

INDEX

Acceleration clause 53–54
Annual Percentage Rate
    (APR) 29, 103, 106–107

Balance remaining 23,
    26–27
Balloon Payment 23, 26
Banks
  Commercial 33, 94
  Mutual Savings 32–33
Beneficiary 48–49, 95

Certificate
  of Intention 89
  of Reasonable Value
    (CRV) 52, 86, 87
  of Veterans Status 67–68
Closing Costs (FHA) 65–66
Compound amount 28
Condominiums
  builders shifting to 10
  FHA program for 74
Credit Unions 34

Default 94, 98
  by veteran 52
  Notice of 49
  on land contract 51
Depression 9, 31–32
Discount 100, 102, 111
  loans 53
  sell at 38
Dollars
  deflated 9, 46
Due-on-sale clause 54,
    94

Equity of Redemption 49
European countries
home finance in 8
interest rate in 8

Fee 52, 110
assumption 94
commitment 58
loan 34–35, 38, 53, 66
Federal Deposit Insurance Corps. (FDIC) 33
Federal Funds Rate 18
Federal Home Loan Bank Board 32
FHA (Federal Housing Administration) 34
Financing programs covered 61–84
Federal National Mortgage Assoc. (FNMA)
as a secondary market 39, 87
auction yield rate 18
Federal Reserve Bank 16–17
Federal Savings and Loan Insurance Corp. 32
Finance charge 29, 103, 106–107
Financial disclosure 103–108
Financing
conventional 45, 49
future of home 10
interim 47
market for seconds 102
no money down 99–100
secondary 49–50, 99, 101
sources for secondary 101
sources of real estate 31
types of FHA 61–84
VA 85
Foreclosure 48–49

Government National Mortgage Assoc. (GNMA) 39, 87

Home Loan Companies 35

Inflation
rate of 9–10, 46, 50
Insurance
Private mortgage 34
Insurance companies 33, 94
Interest
add-on 27–29
comparing add-on to simple 28–29
compound 28
computation of simple 22–23
odd days 26
rates defined 16
rates of 17, 38
reduce effective rate of 9
simple 21–24, 27–29
tax deductibility of 9

Land
foundation for prosperity 7
Land Contract 51, 95, 97, 99

Leverage
  Borrowed Money and 115–116
Lien 45
Liquidity 39
Loan
  amortized 23–24, -6, 30, 42, 48
  assume a 52, 97–98
  chattel 54
  commercial 55
  commitments 47, 57–59
  construction 55
  farm 46
  FHA 32, 45, 52–53, 94
  guaranty (VA) 86
  home improvement 55
  personal 55
  refinance or take out a second 41
  seasoned 39, 53, 87
  VA 32, 45, 51–53, 94
  VA & FHA assumption 52, 99
Loan brokers 35–38

Mobile home
  FHA financing for 83–84
  Parks, FHA financing for 68–69
  VA financing for 91
Money market
  functioning of 22, 38–39
Money supply 15–16, 18
  tighten the 18
Mortgage 45–46, 48
  assuming a 54, 93–94
  construction 47
  contract 46
  conventional 47
  Graduated Payment (FHA) 78–82
  insurance (FHA) 64
  note 46
  open-end 46
  second 49
  taking subject to a 93–94
  variable rate 46
  with release clause 47
Mortgage Bankers 34
Mortgage Companies 35, 58
Mortgagee 46, 48
Mortgagor 46, 48

Points 52, 66, 90
  discount 53, 87
Power of sale 48
Prepayment penalty 54, 90, 94
Prime rate 17–18
Principal 24, 28–30, 38, 41, 51, 102

Rate
  discounted 39
Real estate
  appreciate 10
  brokers as loan brokers 36
Regulation Z 29, 103–105, 107–108
Rule of 78 Rebate 27

Savings and loan associations 31–32, 39, 50, 94

Tight money 51, 59
Treasury Bill Rate 17
Trust deed 46, 48
  all inclusive 95–98
  overlapping 95
  second 49
Trust fund 67
Trustee 48–49
Trustor 48–49, 95
Tycoon 7, 116

United States
  requirements for home
    finance 8

Veteran's Administration
    51, 87

Yield 53, 102, 109–112,
    115–116
  effective on AITD 96
  on FNMA auction 18
  on T-bills 17